SILAS
JAYNE

SILAS
JAYNE

CHICAGO'S SUBURBAN GANGSTER

Bryan Alaspa

Charleston — London

THE
History
PRESS

Published by The History Press
Charleston, SC 29403
www.historypress.net

Unless otherwise noted, all photographs are taken by the author.

First published 2010

Manufactured in the United States

ISBN 978 1.59629.968.9

Library of Congress Cataloging-in-Publication Data

Alaspa, Bryan.
Silas Jayne : Chicago's suburban gangster / Bryan Alaspa.
p. cm.
Includes bibliographical references.
ISBN 978-1-59629-968-9
1. Jayne, Silas, 1907-1987. 2. Gangsters--Illinois--Chicago--Biography. 3. Murderers--
Illinois--Chicago--Biography. 4. Murder--Illinois--Chicago--Case studies. I. Title.
HV6248.J36A43 2010
364.152'3092--dc22
[B]
2010022412

For Melanie, who inspired me, pushed me and helped me
more than anyone could possibly know

CONTENTS

ACKNOWLEDGEMENTS

I wanted to thank the work of writer Gene O'Shea. His article for *Chicago Magazine* entitled "Blood Feud" and his book *Unbridled Rage: A True Story of Organized Crime, Corruption, and Murder in Chicago* were invaluable. Just in helping keep the timelines of the various crimes of Silas Jayne, his work was important. I could not have written this book without him.

I also want to thank Troy Taylor, a fellow History Press author who has a website called Prairie Ghosts that provided important information on the Schuessler-Peterson murders.

Finally, although the book is dedicated to her, I also want to thank Melanie Parker. She helped me in more ways than anyone could imagine. Her tireless efforts in pushing me to finish this project made it all possible. I cannot ever thank her enough.

A CITY BUILT ON BLOOD

When the body of Silas Jayne was brought out of the hospital, the people who were the most surprised at how he died were those who had been investigating and watching him for years. Silas Jayne had fooled all of them by dying peacefully in his sleep. Given the life he had led and the things he was convicted of and suspected of doing, a far more violent ending seemed in the cards.

Chicago is a city that seems built on blood. The history of this metropolis is built on the blood of innocents. It started with a fort that turned into a massacre, and from there, the blood just seemed to keep flowing. The fort was Fort Dearborn, and it was, at one time, at the farthest edge of the frontier of the United States. It was also deep in what was then Native American territory. In fact, it was so deep that many tribes that might have fought against one another instead united in their hatred and disapproval of the fort. Ultimately, the tension grew until multiple tribes surrounded the fort.

What happened then was a bloodbath. The tribes tricked the settlers into thinking they were going to be let go, and then they ambushed the soldiers and settlers. The descriptions of the brutality inflicted upon those soldiers and settlers has become legendary. The ground was, very literally, soaked in blood. It was, ultimately, a losing battle for the Native Americans. The fort eventually became a town. That town grew and became a city. Before long, it had become a boomtown and a huge city.

However, the blood continued to flow. No sooner had the settlement become a city then there was the great fire, which tore through downtown Chicago and killed hundreds. However, the city rebuilt itself, and not too terribly long after the city was nearly destroyed, it hosted the World's Fair. At the same time the city was showing itself off to the world, a man named H.H. Holmes was continuing that trail of blood. As the world marveled at a city that had rebuilt itself, he was building a hotel designed almost solely for murdering women. When his crimes were discovered, the city, and much of the world, was shocked at the cruelty and depravity he had displayed.

Still, the city continued to grow. However, the city was also growing a reputation. It was a city known for being brutal. The South Side of the city was filled with slaughterhouses where the blood of animals ran freely and soaked the ground. Carl Sandburg's novel about working in those houses, *The Jungle*, showed just how brutal life there was.

Of course, if you ask most people who have never been to Chicago what they know about the city, they will tell you they know about the snow, some sports legends and a certain gangster with a scar on his face. The name Al Capone, as much as many modern city officials wish it were not so, is forever linked to the city of Chicago. During the time that Al Capone held the city of Chicago in his hands, he was notorious for his brutality. It was rumored that the "mob" on the East Coast wanted nothing to do with the Chicago outfit because they considered the Midwesterners barbarians. The St. Valentine's Day Massacre was Capone's masterstroke and was so brutal that it shocked the city and started to turn many who supported him against him.

Once the gangster era passed, Chicago grew again. It had become, first, a center for railways and then for air traffic. The downtown area expanded into the lake, and the buildings stretched farther and farther into the sky. However, there was still that feeling of Chicago being a tough town. There were those still creating those rivers of blood that seemed to create the very lifeforce for the city to survive.

Some of the names of the city's most notorious bloodletters have become famous. John Wayne Gacy murdered some thirty-five young men, that are known. Even worse, he tortured them before he killed them and then buried many of them in the crawlspace beneath his own home. Gacy held the dubious honor of being the country's most prolific serial killer for some time.

The name Richard Speck is also well known. He came well before Gacy and shocked the city and the nation by murdering student nurses in their apartments during one night that turned into an orgy of murder. He carefully, methodically and brutally bound, raped and murdered eight student nurses. He even had the words "Born to Raise Hell" tattooed on his arm.

The names of Capone, Gacy and Speck have become legendary in the annals of crime. They have become famous boogeymen for parents and people to scare their children or those prone to being scared. Of the many crimes and criminals, they are probably the three most famous.

However, the entire Chicago metropolitan area is a lot more than the city itself. Chicago and its suburbs stretch out for many miles in all directions. Within those areas there have been criminals, too. Perhaps because they were not in downtown Chicago, they have not become well known. Even among those who lived and did their dirty work in the 'burbs, there is a name that should rank among the most infamous and brutal killers the world has ever seen. That name is Silas Jayne.

Silas Jayne was as cold and brutal as Capone on his worst day. He ordered the killing of people and their entire families with the ease of ordering a cheeseburger at a hamburger stand. He was not above brutalizing women, children and even his own family. These days, those who feel little or no remorse for the crimes they commit are known as sociopaths. Had Silas Jayne lived in different times, he would have been given that label and perhaps been treated for his illness. Since he did not, however, he committed his crimes almost without reprisal for a very long time.

One thing that Silas Jayne was very good at was keeping secrets. Yes, he was ultimately put in prison for at least one of his crimes, but the bulk of the horrific deeds he had been part of did not come out until well after his death. Law enforcement knew or suspected him in a variety of crimes. Those who did live and work in the western suburbs of Chicago or those who knew anything about horses knew the name of Silas Jayne. He had a knack for being charming. He was known as "Si" to his friends.

He was known for being crude but charming and had a sense of humor that would make many of his friends laugh and say, "Oh, that's just Si."

However, the day he was carried from the hospital, having died peacefully in his sleep, was the day that the dam of silence began to break. Soon, people who had been terrified of reprisals began to talk about Silas Jayne. It was then that the full scope of his crimes became evident.

Perhaps because he did his dirty work in the suburbs, the name of Silas Jayne has not reached the fame and infamy of Capone, Gacy or Speck. However, his crimes were no less brutal and no less bloody. He deserves his spot on the criminal podium. He was a horseman, but he was also a brute. He was Silas Jayne, and he was Chicago's suburban gangster.

CHAPTER 1

THE EARLY YEARS

He Had Cold Eyes

It would have been something you could point to and say that there was something wrong if Silas Jayne had been born with horns, scaly red skin and a forked tail. Had he been born with fangs and yellow cat's eyes, someone might have been able to point to the child and see the potential for evil that was there. However, life never quite works the way it does in the movies. No, there was nothing remarkable about Silas Jayne's birth. There was nothing to indicate what he would become or the harm he would cause.

The man who would become the terror of the horse world was born to Arthur and Katherine Jayne on July 3, 1907. The Jayne family reportedly could trace its lineage all the way back to colonial times. To add to the family's strangely patriotic feel, Silas was nearly born on Independence Day. Silas was the first of four boys in a family that would ultimately have twelve children. If there was anything in his early days that might have given pause to anyone looking at his life at that time, it would have been his father. By all accounts, Arthur was far from the best role model for a group of young men.

Arthur Jayne was a man who, according to records from the time, had a variety of jobs, and not all of them were legal. Some of the jobs on his resume were farmer, stockyard worker and truck driver. One of his more lucrative careers was supplying sugar to bootleggers during Prohibition. He was reportedly a man of surly disposition, and he was not afraid to take out his frustrations on his family. Arthur was reportedly an alcoholic. Exactly what he may have done to his family is not entirely known. It is known that, eventually, Katherine decided she had had enough and separated from Arthur. It is also known that he did not do much to encourage his children, especially his oldest son Silas, to stay in school and do something with their lives.

The Jaynes lived on a farm, and the Jayne children worked that farm rather than focusing on school. Their farm was near a lake, and upon that lake were numerous geese and other waterfowl that were known to wander the family farm. Perhaps it was a crossing with these geese that let the world, or at least the Jayne family, see the darkness that was lurking beneath Silas's face. Perhaps it gave them a peek into the rage and violence that bubbled just below the surface.

There are no documents to support what would become a Jayne family legend, but it is a story told so often that there must be some kernel of truth to it. The fact that the story has been handed down from one family member to the next means that the exact details of the story have been lost to history. Whether Silas was six or eight years old seems a moot point; regardless, he was very young and of an age when most boys would be afraid of being attacked by a goose or any animal. If a normal, well-adjusted boy was attacked by any animal, it would not have been surprising for that boy to cry and perhaps run away. Silas was not such a boy.

The story goes that Silas was walking near the lake on the family farm. The flock of geese was in the water, and some, like has been known to happen with geese, also walked around on the grass, their beaks pecking away at the tall blades looking for tiny morsels to eat. As they honked and strutted, their long necks dipping into both water and grass, Silas Jayne, a young boy with cold, dark eyes and a curly mop of hair, came strolling by.

Geese are, by nature, very territorial animals. Most often they are seen in large groups around bodies of water. As most of the flock looks for food, there are always a few that guard the perimeter. They often issue hissing warnings to those who are wandering too close and then continue to threaten. Then the geese are known to attack, spreading their impressive wings and charging the potential threat, using their sharp beaks to peck and attack as needed.

Silas must have been perceived as a threat. Whatever warnings were given by the geese doing the guarding must have been ignored or were not understood by the young boy. Silas ended up being bitten, and bitten hard. Again, being the tender age he was, it would not have been unusual for him to run home in tears. It would not have been unusual for him to scream in pain. Just about any reaction other than the one Silas had probably would have been considered closer to normal.

Silas Jayne did not cry. He did not scream. Instead, according to his family, he walked calmly back to the house and grabbed an axe. He then calmly walked back to the goose that had bitten him and hacked the bird to pieces. Covered in the blood of the bird he had just slaughtered, Silas was not yet satisfied. He looked out over the lake at the rest of the flock, and he channeled his rage and waded into them with his axe swinging. How long it took is unknown, but what is known, according to his family, is that Silas wiped out the entire flock, leaving bleeding, hacked and chopped bird carcasses in his path of vengeance. He then ran home, his body, face and clothes covered with the clotting blood of maybe a dozen or more birds and feathers caught in his hair. Was he sorry? Did he cry out in fear for what he had just done? No. Reportedly, he excitedly and proudly told his family what he had done.

Today, of course, such a thing would be greeted with shock. People would spread the rumor of the vicious child who hacked a flock of geese into pieces and then bragged about it. Cruelty to animals is now recognized as a sign of deep mental problems inside the mind of a child and is a sign of a sociopath. A child today would likely end up in headlines at least in local papers, and charges of animal cruelty would be filed. The parents of a child who did such a thing today would be referred to child psychologists, and medication would be prescribed. None of that happened, of course, in the early 1900s, when Silas did his deed. In fact, this started a kind of family and friend of the family trend that would continue throughout Silas's life.

"That was just Si," is what so many who knew him or were related to him would say when he said or did something outrageous. Given what his father was, maybe he even saw the fact that Silas did not cry and took care of business on his own as a badge of honor. Whatever did happen among his family, he was not seen as sick and was not taken to doctors for treatment. It should have been a warning, but it was ignored.

Silas and his brothers continued to work on the family farm. Education was not a key concern to his father. Silas would drop out of school by the time the ninth grade rolled around. He did not know how to read and could not sign his name, but he was already showing signs of being a shrewd and intelligent businessman.

Eventually, Silas's mother, Katherine, had had enough of Arthur, his drinking and his tendency toward crime and things unsavory. She did not divorce him, but they separated in the early 1920s. What happened to Arthur is not generally known, but what Silas's mother did is known because it would become key for Silas and, in many ways, alter his life forever.

Katherine needed a job, and she found one by working for a man named George Spunner. Spunner made his living as a lawyer, but he also supplemented his income by running a kind of summer vacation camp on Lake Zurich in Illinois. He managed a number of cabins that vacationers could rent and use during the summer months and enjoy time with nature and swimming in the lake. She helped clean and maintain the cabins as well as working in the office. She also developed a very noticeable liking to George Spunner.

Compared to what she had endured with Arthur, George must have seemed like a knight in shining armor. He helped people using his law firm, and he was wise enough to invest in things like property and the campground. Although hardly a multimillionaire, he was much more stable and well off than the drunken Arthur, who seemed to take any and all jobs he could get his hands on. It was only a matter of time before George noticed Katherine in return, and a romance developed.

Silas and his siblings were living with his mother at that time. It is likely that Si, being as clever as he was, knew what was happening. Exactly what he thought of it remains a mystery, but the result of the affair was obvious and would lead to a key part of Silas's life.

Katherine gave birth to another boy on November 2, 1923. She called the boy George but gave him the last name of Jayne. It is likely that this was an attempt to cover up the affair and protect herself, her family and the family and reputation of George Spunner.

Silas and George did not exactly get along like Silas and the rest of his brothers. Silas was particularly close to his brother DeForest, who, despite being younger, managed to have a calming and focusing effect on Silas. He seemed able to corral the tendency for wildness and violence that brewed beneath the surface of Silas's features. His half brother George, meanwhile, seemed only to serve as a reminder to Silas that George may have been from better stock. Certainly, things happened throughout George's life that only seemed to reaffirm that belief.

Silas had his first real run-in with the law at the age of seventeen. It was another glimpse into the darkness and brutality that lay beneath his handsome face and cold, dark eyes. It should have, like the incident with the geese, served as a warning to all involved, but again, like the geese, it seemed to have the opposite effect.

According to reports, Silas was driving into town, perhaps to meet friends or just hang out, when he saw a young girl walking on the side of the road. Silas had an eye for the ladies, and he pulled over, slowing the car to a crawl. He rolled down the window and struck up a conversation with the girl. He invited her to go with him into town. He promised her that they would visit a local soda fountain and enjoy an ice cream soda together. It seemed innocent enough. The girl accepted.

Even at that young age, the Jayne family was starting to gain fame in their town. They had started to get into horses. They were rounding up horses and training them for rodeos. What must that girl have thought when Silas pulled up and asked her out? Everyone knew the Jayne boys were a little wild at times and rough around the edges, but they were manly and exciting. They were strong and handsome. They were cowboys. By the same token, what demons lurked beneath the mop of curly hair atop Silas's head? What did his cold eyes hide? Somewhere along the way, that young girl found out what was there.

They did not make it into town. Instead, Silas found a deserted road in the woods and parked the car. Somehow, he dragged the girl into the back seat. Once there, he raped her. Once again, Silas Jayne proved he had little to no regard for anyone else and that what he wanted, he simply got.

However, he did not get away with this one. He was arrested, as the girl went to the police. Silas was brought up on juvenile rape charges. Silas found himself defended by none other than the father of his half brother, George Spunner. According to those who have talked about the case since then, George Spunner apparently had little regard for the young man who liked to get into fights and had done this to a young girl. He did not mount much of a defense. In fact, it has been reported that he talked to the judge and determined that time in prison might "do Si some good."

Silas Jayne, age seventeen, was sentenced to a year in jail. It may have been the hope of George Spunner that Silas would be scared straight by what he saw behind bars. Maybe he thought Silas would learn his lesson and decide that a life of crime was not worth the potential punishment. Whatever he thought he would learn, George Spunner was very wrong. The Silas Jayne who emerged from prison a year later was a hardened man with a grudge against his half brother, George. While the grudge may have been small at that point, the seeds were planted and planted deep, and they would blossom into violence later on.

Silas Jayne joined with his brothers and began to focus on horses and his riding. All of the brothers were natural horsemen, as if riding was just in their blood. Even George was talented at riding horses. They began performing rodeo shows, traveling around the state and drawing crowds.

There were problems with Silas, however, as the brothers traveled about and rode their horses. He liked to drink, and it didn't matter what his age was or whether the average person was supposed to have access to alcohol. The demons inside him continued to manifest in violence, and the mixture of drinks and those demons meant that Silas continued to have more run-ins with the law. Most of the incidents were minor and involved fines and short stays in local county jails, but it was evidence that something rotten was brewing beneath the surface. Still, his brothers Frank and DeForest managed to keep him under control, and the incidents never got too wild.

In 1927, Silas decided he wanted to get married. The name of his first wife is not even known, and Silas barely spoke of this woman in coming years. The marriage only lasted six months, and the only thing Silas would say later on was that it was a mistake.

The brothers were still gaining a reputation around town. They were known for meeting a train at the depot and unloading a load of horses. They would then lead those hundreds of horses through the center of town to their stables at the far end of town. It created quite a spectacle. Once the horses were in the stables, some of the horses were trained for their rodeo and others were sent off to slaughter to be turned into dog food.

All of the brothers were known to be a little rough around the edges. It was common knowledge that you did not want to get mixed up with the "Jesse Jayne Gang." They were cowboys long past the time of cowboys, and they became notorious and respected.

One thing is known, and that is all of the brothers had business sense. They were making money buying and selling horses. They knew a good opportunity when they saw one. Eventually, all of the brothers would open up their own stables and run their own businesses, to various levels of success. Silas opened his first stables in 1932. Shortly after that, tragedy struck the Jayne family. Unfortunately for Silas, and for those around him, that tragedy befell the one brother who seemed to have any kind of calming effect on Silas: DeForest.

DeForest Jayne had the same rugged good looks of his brothers. He was also a bit rough, but from all accounts, he was one of the calmer brothers. He was practical, and the wild demons that inhabited his older brother had passed him by. It was only a matter of time before he would meet and fall in love with someone. The woman's name was Mae Sweeney. DeForest fell head over heels in love with her, and they were a perfect couple. Not long after their courtship started, they were engaged.

What DeForest didn't know was that something dark lurked beneath the surface of his beloved. It was not the same kind of darkness that lurked in his brother, but it would have devastating consequences. Mae Sweeney loved DeForest, but she was prone to depression.

One night shortly after the two were engaged, DeForest left his home to go visit his sweetheart. They were scheduled to go out on a date that night. However, DeForest was not aware of the fact that shortly after they had made their plans, Mae had taken a large dose of arsenic and died in her room. DeForest found her on the floor, lifeless, and his heart was broken.

DeForest was devastated. His brothers could tell that he was destroyed and saddened beyond anything they had seen in him before. He managed to get through the funeral and then went back to his home. The brothers and the rest of the family did not hear from him for a while, and they began to get worried.

Silas and Frank decided they were going to try to cheer up their saddened brother. They left their homes, met up and headed over to DeForest's home. There was no answer when they knocked on the door. They could see no life inside the home as they walked around the house. They began searching all of the potential places that DeForest might have been. Soon, the rest of the Jayne family was looking, and with each passing hour, their concern grew greater. Finally, after searching every place they could think of, they went to the one place they hoped they would not find DeForest— the cemetery.

Frank and Silas walked through the silent graveyard together. They encouraged their sisters to stay away from the scene, and they walked over and past the quiet graves. They finally stopped at Mae's grave site. The earth there was still barren, still fresh, from the recent funeral.

The brothers saw what they had feared the most. Lying next to the grave was the body of their dear brother DeForest. "D," as he was known, had gone home and, somewhere along the line, taken a shotgun and made his way back to the cemetery where his beloved Mae lay beneath the earth. He then put the shotgun into his mouth and pulled the trigger.

The last thing that had been able to keep Silas in check was now gone. Silas, meanwhile, had met and fallen in love with another woman. Her name was Martha, and they eventually married in 1938. At first, Martha had a positive effect on Silas. While it wasn't quite the same thing as the effect DeForest had, she did settle him down long enough to teach him how to read and sign his name.

The calming effect did not last long. In 1940, a suspicious fire broke out in a barn owned by Silas. Inside were many horses, and as the flames leapt higher and higher, ten of them perished. Although the authorities were dubious about the cause of the fire, they had no reason to arrest or charge Silas or his brothers with anything. Silas collected a sizable insurance settlement on the stable and the animals. Thus, one of the

Jayne Gang's favorite scams was born and would be played and replayed again and again throughout the years.

By now, Silas had a stable where he was teaching young women how to ride. It was a way for him to indulge himself in one of his hobbies, which was hitting on and seducing young girls. However, he was very good at convincing the fathers of these young girls that they needed riding lessons and a horse.

In 1941, Silas had his first real run-in with the law as an adult, ending up in court. One of his riding students, Ruth DeWar, brought Silas into court and sued him for bodily harm. She claimed that Silas had deliberately spooked a horse she was riding on and the animal had reared up, sending her tumbling off. She had fractured her spine and was in tremendous pain.

Silas was charged and ended up in court. He sat there and stared at the all-female jury. He made sure to look each and every juror in the eye, staring at them and, seemingly, through them. Reportedly, the jurors were completely unnerved by his cold, seemingly endless stare. Silas was found not guilty.

As the war years came, the Jayne brothers found new scams and new ways to make money. Since beef was now being rationed, restaurants and eateries were desperate for meat. The Jaynes had horses, and when they were slaughtered and their bodies ground up, it looked and tasted enough like beef for most eateries. So the Jayne Gang began selling horsemeat to restaurants as beef. Since most restaurants were desperate enough to use horsemeat and deal with unsavory characters like Silas to get meat, it was a mutually beneficial business transaction.

Silas's empire was starting to grow after the death of his brother. He began to open more and more stables in and around the northwest suburbs of Chicago. His list of clients and students began to grow as well. His tendency to attract unsavory people and to keep them under his wing also began to develop. Before too long, others were noticing his business, and they wanted in on it.

Of course, Chicago is famous for being a Mafia city. Al Capone had run the mob during Prohibition. He was long gone, however, by the time World War II came along. Still, his right-hand man, Tony Accardo, had taken over and ruled the city with his infamous iron fist. He had been a bodyguard for Capone and was known for his ruthlessness. Before too long, the mob was taking a notice in Silas and others who owned stables.

One of the things that the mob liked to do was use legitimate businesses as "fronts." In particular, they liked to use the barns and stables in the far suburbs as brothels. Before too long, Silas was approached about his stables and turning them, or at least some of them, into brothels. At least one is known to have been turned into a brothel, but Silas had a way of keeping the mob at arm's length. However, Silas would have to deal with the mob throughout his life and they would, at times, be useful for him.

Not long after Silas agreed to let the mob use one of his stables as a house of ill repute, he committed his first murder. This is a tale told, again, by family members, although no evidence has ever actually been brought forward to prove that he did anything. The tale goes that, in 1947, a man from the mob approached Silas in one of his stables. The reason for the visit remains shrouded in mystery. Some believe he was a collector and he was there to collect on a debt or perhaps a tax owed to a mob boss. It is believed that Silas lured the man into the barn and then killed him.

In the mafia, no one gets killed unless it is approved by someone higher up. So either Silas had killed the man on orders from someone up higher or it was an act of true defiance. Perhaps he wanted to send a clear message to the mob that he could live with them and do business with them, but they could not push him around.

The body was reportedly chopped up and disposed of. No one ever saw the man again, and the truth of the matter, again, became family legend. That was Si, and that was what he did. He was ruthless and he wouldn't let anyone push him around.

For most of the rest of his life, the mob left Silas alone. He was allowed to run his scams and schemes in the suburbs, while the mob handled things in the big city and other areas. Silas was too unstable even for the famously brutal Chicago mafia. It was as if both sides decided to just stay out of each other's way.

Silas had scams and cons that he had started to perfect. Now that he was buying and selling horses and not doing as much rodeo riding of his own, he developed a scam involving the young women and girls whom he taught how to ride. This led to a con that he would commit again and again throughout the rest of his life. In fact, it was a con that he would teach others who entered his orbit.

The scam was fairly simple. Silas's stables were set up in the predominantly wealthy northwest suburbs of Chicago. Generally, the families who lived out there, particularly at that time, had plenty of money and owned large estates. Most of them also had families that included young daughters. It was considered a sign of wealth and prestige to sign their young daughters up for riding lessons. Since Silas had some of the most famous and predominant stables, and a reputation in the area, he was often the choice of these wealthy families.

The scam then went into effect. Silas would train the girl for a period of time. When the fathers and families would ask for a progress report on their daughter, Silas would turn on the charm. He would praise their daughter's abilities at riding. He would then suggest that she had real talent and could go far in the riding world, but to do so, they would have to buy her a horse of her own that she could then learn from and go farther with. With a daughter looking on with pleading eyes, most fathers were destined to give in and pay for a horse, which, of course, Silas Jayne would help them pick out. This is where the second part of the scam would come in.

Silas had begun assembling a number of veterinarians in the area to certify his horses. However, the horses he wanted certified as healthy and, therefore, expensive were horses that were nowhere near that quality. In fact, he would often have horses that were a hair's breadth away from the glue factory certified as perfectly healthy. Silas was very persuasive when it came to getting these horse doctors on his side. Anyone who refused him would find his property set on fire. In one case, a vet had not only refused but also threatened to turn Silas into the authorities, and a bomb went off on his property. His house was damaged and no one was killed, but the message got through. The horses were certified, and any legal proceedings that had started were stopped.

So, these fathers, wanting only to please their teary-eyed daughters and give them every chance, often found themselves in a tough situation. Silas would try to sell them horses at premium prices that were nowhere near worth that amount. Some fathers had no idea about horses and would simply pay. Silas also had a plan for those fathers who maybe knew more about horses than the average man. When he ran into a father who knew the horse he was buying wasn't worth the money Silas was asking, Silas would use blackmail. He would say that the daughter had been flirting with members of his staff and stable hands. He would sometimes say that she had been having sex with stable workers or even Silas himself. He would then threaten to let that information out and start rumors that would damage the family's reputation. Of course, in the wealthy and close-knit society of the rich in the northwest suburbs, such a thing would have been devastating for the young women. The fathers would then open their checkbooks or wallets. At that time, none would dare try going to the police either.

Of course, the worst part of it all was that Silas often did have sex with these young women. He was not particularly shy about it, either, and would often brag to his friends and employees. He called it "funnin' with them."

Silas, as has been mentioned before, had a knack for attracting the worst that society had to offer. It was as if he were some kind of dark, poisonous sun that drew other dark and poisonous people to his orbit. He would take them under his wing, teach them his cons and sometimes set them loose to run their own operations without him. Of course, Silas always got his cut, but he took a certain pride in teaching the horrible things he had learned to others.

Silas was not above showing off his wealth. He wore a huge pinky ring on one hand. He had a twenty-dollar gold piece turned into a belt buckle. He bought a new Cadillac every year and would outfit the hood of each with the horns of a steer.

However, as the 1940s ended and the supposedly innocent time of the '50s came about, Silas would become involved in a crime so horrendous that it would haunt the Chicago area for over forty years. It was a crime that many considered the final blow to whatever innocence this city, with its long and bloody history, might have had left. It was a crime that slapped the city across the face and made parents keep their children closer. Finally, it was a crime that would show just how terrifying Silas Jayne was. Because this crime, and his involvement in it, would not become evident until long after he was dead. Silas Jayne knew how to make sure his secrets were kept.

It was a crime that involved three young boys, and it would become one of the most famous unsolved crimes in Chicago history for almost half a century.

CHAPTER 2

THE MURDER
OF THREE YOUNG BOYS

The day was October 16, 1955, and it was gray and rainy. It was a different time and day than it is today. It was a time much more naïve than today. Even in Chicago, a city that had seen so much crime and pain and blood, things were still done differently than today. It was not uncommon for parents to let their children out on their own, all day long, to head downtown to see movies or hang out. This was the world that John and Anton Schuessler and Bobby Peterson were used to. However, October 16, 1955, was the last day that those boys would be seen alive.

That morning, John, age thirteen, and Anton, age eleven, spent their time at home. The day was predicting rain, and they had plans to visit their friend Bobby Peterson and then head downtown. They told their parents that they were going to see the new Disney movie, *The African Lion*.

The two boys set off on their bicycles for Bobby's home at 2:30 p.m. They arrived at the Peterson home a few minutes later. The three boys spent time talking with Malcolm Peterson, Bobby's father, and discussing their plans for the rest of the day. Eventually they decided it was time to make their way to the train or bus so that they could get downtown. At 3:00 p.m., they left the house of Bobby Peterson and headed off on their bicycles.

Instead of heading straight for the movie, the three boys eventually met up with their mutual friends Bruce and Glen Carter. They shared a bottle of Green River soda and stood in a nearby alley. The boys talked about their plans for the day, and Bobby mentioned that they had plans to head out to Idle Hour Stable to ride some horses. The Carter brothers were familiar with the Idle Hour Stables, and they knew how much fun it was to ride horses there. They asked if they could go with the boys, but the Schuesslers and Bobby Peterson stated that the invitation was for them only because they knew someone who worked at the stable. At one point, a car drove past the opening of the alley where the boys were standing and honked twice.

Anton looked at the car and asked, "Is that Hansen?"

John nudged him and said, "Be quiet, we've said too much already."

Bruce Carter was confused. He stared down the alley at the vehicle, because he had a cousin named Hansen and he wondered if he might be old enough to have gotten his driver's license. As he moved toward the car, it drove off. Then John Schuessler took the soda bottle and smashed it against the wall, causing such noise that the boys ran away. The Carter brothers did not see the boys again, but the whole incident stayed in their minds and became important later.

At 3:55 p.m., the weather reports and meteorological data for that day show that it started to rain. It continued to rain the rest of that afternoon and evening. Again, this would become very important later.

The three boys eventually did make it downtown to see the Disney movie. At 7:15 p.m., the three of them were seen at the Monte Cristo Bowling Alley by a man named Ernest Niewiadomski and his two sisters. He recognized them from the neighborhood and approached them to say hello. He had a brief conversation with the boys, and they told him about *The African Lion*. Their conversation was short, and eventually Ernest went back to hanging out with his sisters and bowling.

At 8:00 p.m., a man named Harold Blumfield was driving back home. He saw three boys on the side of the road attempting to hitchhike. He pulled over, let the three boys into his car and gave them a ride from Kimball Avenue in Chicago to 4444 Montrose Avenue. This spot was not far from where the boys lived.

At 8:40 p.m., three boys who matched the description of John, Anton and Bobby were seen at the Garden Bowling Alley by several witnesses who reported the sighting after the crime made the headlines in the following days. There was some debate as to how long the boys were at the alley.

At 8:47 p.m., Bruno Mencarini was driving his Chicago Transit Authority bus down the street and pulled over to let on three boys. He later told police that he was certain these boys were the Schuessler and Peterson boys. He said that they were on his bus for a short time and stated that they left the bus at 8:52 p.m.

At 9:00 p.m., a man named George Kimske and his wife were driving home and saw three boys hitchhiking at Lawrence Avenue. At the same time, a man named Ralph Helm was walking down the street when he saw John, Anton and Bobby. Ralph also knew the boys from the neighborhood, but he didn't think there was anything strange about these, or any other, young men hitchhiking in the neighborhood at that time of night. He waved to the boys, and he and his friends walked past one another and then on into the night.

From 9:15 p.m. to midnight, the boys were not seen again. There were no more reports of them being seen anywhere around the neighborhood. In fact, the three young men were not seen alive again. However, this is not the end of the strange things seen or heard that night.

At 9:15 p.m. in the northwest suburb of Park Ridge, Illinois, a man named Stanely Panek was out walking his dog. He lived right next door to Idle Hour Stable, and he heard strange noises coming from them. He would later tell police that he heard something that sounded like someone "beating the hell out of a child." He also said that he heard what sounded like a child screaming.

At 11:00 p.m., a Delores Wisilinski, who also lived in Park Ridge near the Idle Hour Stables, said that she heard screaming as well. She claimed that she heard someone screaming, "No! No!" and then she heard an adult voice, very angry, saying, "Get in there!" Finally, she claimed, not long after the screaming stopped, she heard a car driving away at high speed.

At the same time, another neighbor, Mrs. Walter Grzybowski, told police that her dog was very agitated. This was unlike her dog, and she was concerned. At about midnight, she let the dog out, and the dog kept looking at the same spot in a field that was part of the Idle Hour Stables.

That is the last known report of anything that may or may not have been connected to the crime committed against the three boys. Nothing else was heard or seen. When the boys failed to return home, Malcolm Peterson contacted a friend of his on the police force. He was worried. Anton Schuessler Sr. was also worried, and he and his wife also contacted the police. For the next several days, it was considered a missing persons case.

It seemed as if the boys had simply vanished from the face of the earth. The police began to comb the area. Pictures of the three missing boys began to show up in the local media, along with descriptions of what the boys were wearing. John was wearing blue jeans and a tan belt. He was also wearing a brown cotton long-sleeved shirt with a western theme. He had a satin Chicago Cubs jacket as well as black and white gym shoes and white socks. John's younger brother, Anton Jr., also known as Tony, was wearing a tattered Cubs jacket. He also had a white flannel long-sleeved shirt with a black wavey pattern across the front. He had on tattered blue jeans and black and white gym shoes with blue socks. Bobby Peterson was wearing a black satin Chicago White Sox jacket. He also wore a flannel shirt beneath the jacket. He had blue jeans on that were patched in two places and a multicolored beaded belt. He topped his outfit off with white boxers, a white T-shirt and black canvas high-tops.

Then, on October 18, 1955, the discovery that no one wanted was made. A man parked his car near a forest preserve when he thought he saw something strange from his car. As he moved closer, he thought he saw three mannequins tossed by the side of the road. However, it became more and more obvious that these were not mannequins. The man made a call to the police and reported that there were three bodies near the Robinson Woods Forest Preserve.

That day and those events set into motion one of the most notorious crimes in the history of Chicago. In a city that was used to crime and had already seen some truly horrible things, the fact that this crime involved three innocent children murdered so heinously and then discarded like trash shocked the entire city and electrified the citizenry. Nothing was ever the same for parents and children in the city. The permissive nature of parents would forever be changed. At least one law enforcement official was quoted as saying that if the city was so dangerous that you couldn't let your kids go downtown and see a movie then the city was in too much trouble to save. The days when children would travel, on their own, downtown or wander the city alone or would be caught hitchhiking to get around were pretty much over.

The story hit the newspapers on October 19, 1955. The news was devastating to Anton Schuessler Sr. While his wife, Eleanor, was also devastated, it was Anton Sr. who had to come downtown to identify the bodies of his only two sons. Newspapers captured the moment when the man collapsed while leaving the morgue, held up by his arms by those around him, a look of despair etched across his face.

Almost from the first, however, the investigation was botched. The first problem was who had jurisdiction for the crime. The boys were from Chicago; however, their bodies had been discovered in a suburb. The children were likely abducted, and this meant the Illinois Bureau of Investigation (IBI) was involved. The Cook County sheriff's police were involved. The Chicago Police Department assigned detectives and assembled a taskforce. Other communities surrounding Chicago became involved as the search for evidence spread beyond the forest preserve and into neighboring areas. None of these organizations wanted to communicate with the others. They did not want to share evidence. Some of them hid evidence from other law enforcement divisions. The investigation was in trouble from the start, although police and investigators continued to give statements to the press that they were on the case and likely to find clues and suspects soon.

Immediately after the bodies were found, investigators from all divisions were talking to the press. The first stories in the newspaper show the investigators immediately thought that the three young men had been the victims of an attack by a youth gang. The first statements indicate that investigators thought that the crime matched other crimes they had seen before committed by youth gangs. It was even theorized that the gang might have even been about the same age as the three boys and that they had been "roughed up."

In fact, the boys had been "roughed up," but in ways that shocked even hardened investigators. The three boys had been strangled and beaten severely. Then the bodies had been tossed on the ground, and when they were found, they were still dry. This let investigators know that the bodies had been dumped there after the rain had stopped.

The investigators also, at first, stated that the boys appeared not to have been molested. This became a point of contention many years later and would ultimately be proven wrong. Finally, another unnamed investigator feared that this could be a "thrill kill" crime in the same city that saw the Leopold and Loeb crime only a couple decades before.

The bodies were in a shameful state. Bobby Peterson had apparently put up a struggle with his murderer. He had been repeatedly struck in the head, and the medical examiner found seven wounds in his scalp. Two of those wounds cut down through the outer layer of his skin to his skull. There were finger marks on his neck, but these were ruined by other marks, as if a belt or strap had been wrapped around his throat and twisted. This was what ultimately killed him.

Tony Schuessler had received a particularly hard blow to his left eye. He also had finger marks on his neck. These finger marks were more distinct and visible than on Bobby Peterson, and his life had been choked out of existence by bare hands. Finally, Tony had been punched or struck hard at the base of his skull. Although the blow had not killed him, it had been savage and brutal.

Tony's older brother, John, had received the roughest treatment of all of the boys before he had been mercifully killed. Someone had beaten John so hard that hemorrhages had formed on his brain. He had been punched in the right eye, brutally and hard. His neck had been struck with something so hard that it had completely crushed his windpipe, destroyed his Adam's apple and left his vocal cords inflamed. It was this blow that had killed him by cutting off his air. Finally, and mysteriously, his left thigh had a small hole in it. At first, investigators thought that this had been caused by some kind of rodent or scavenger nibbling on the corpse.

The boys shared some features, however. All three had had their mouths taped shut. Tape had also been placed over their eyes. All three boys showed marks on their wrists that indicated that, at some point, they had been bound.

As for what happened to their clothes, no investigator could say for sure. When the police went to the press, they asked the public to help them search for clues. One of the clues they mentioned was any sign of clothing that looked like it might belong to boys of that age. It was theorized that the killers had kept the clothing as souvenirs, or if they could be found, they might contain some indication of who the killers might be.

Soon after the police first went to the press, they came across what they thought were clues that would break the case wide open. As investigators began doing a search of the surrounding area from where the bodies had been found, they discovered an abandoned car. Inside that car, they found clothing, including blue jeans and shirts that investigators were sure matched the descriptions of the clothing worn by the boys. The clues were so promising that it was reported in the press. However, the parents all denied that the clothing was in any way related to their sons.

Still, it was suspicious, and the parents were inconsolable. So the police ran the license plates of the abandoned car. They were traced back to the owner, who underwent intense questioning for hours, but ultimately, the police were convinced that he had nothing to do with the crime. He was released and vanished from the investigation.

The police then stumbled across another clue they hoped would be particularly enlightening. Scraps of clothing were found deeper in the forest preserve. They thought that the type of material used traced the scraps of clothing back to a local reformatory, and they hoped that would lead them to the killer. Despite initially expressing high hopes to the public over this clue, the scraps of clothing ultimately proved to be a dead end.

The Chicago investigators started their inquest into the disappearance and murders. They brought in everyone who had seen or had any contact with the three boys. First, the parents were questioned. Then, those who had given statements and stated they had seen the boys anytime during that fateful night were questioned. It was eventually realized that none of these people had anything to do with the crime. Things were looking grim already.

Things got worse in the Schuessler home. Anton Schuessler Sr. was going downhill fast. He began to sink into a depression that was beyond profound. He first stopped bathing, and then he stopped changing his clothes. He began staying home, not leaving his house, and he began to get paranoid. His paranoia grew to the point that he was convinced his own family had something to do with the murder of his sons. He became unable to sleep and then started talking about killing himself. His wife and his family became so worried that they had him committed to a sanitarium. He would not emerge.

It was common practice at that time to treat patients of depression with electroshock therapy. Mild courses of electrical current were administered to the temples of the patient, inducing a spasm. As the spasm happened, the brain would release chemicals that, often, would cause the patient to come out of his depression. Anton was such a severe case that it was immediately decided that this was the only course of action available for him. He was brought in, and the shocks were administered. The seizure happened, but the doctors were unable to awaken him. They administered drugs to bring him out of it, but he went into cardiac arrest. Again, more drugs were administered to start his heart, and at first, he seemed to respond. However, he soon had another heart attack, and this time, there was no stopping it. Anton Schuessler died mere weeks after his children. Many say that it was the loss of his boys that did it and that he literally died of a "broken heart."

Eleanor Schuessler had gone from being a wife and mother of two boys to a widow with no children in just a few weeks. She moved away from her home in Chicago and remarried. She even became stepmother to her new husband's children, but those who knew her say that she, too, never really recovered. She may not have died of a broken heart, but she was never the same woman she was before that day.

The police continued to investigate. Initially, tips turned up some promising clues and potential suspects. One of them was a homeless man and vagrant named Richard Fred Ebert. He was known to haunt the area around the forest preserve where the bodies had been found. The police eventually found him and decided to talk to him. Ebert seemed promising at first. He spoke repeatedly about "that time I was in the woods." He also stated that he drank a lot and sometimes had "blackouts" where he would wake up hours or days later and not know where he had been, what he had done or how he had gotten there. However, it soon became clear that he was not the culprit in this crime, despite intense questioning by police.

The funeral for the three boys became a citywide spectacle. Thousands of people showed up at the church and lined the streets. The small coffins were carried through lines of people of all colors, shapes and sizes. More people trailed after them as they were transported to the cemetery and buried. Photos of the coffins and the funeral adorned the numerous newspapers in existence at that time in the Chicago area.

Not long after the bodies were buried, however, the police asked to dig them back up. Their leads had all gone dry, and they wanted to look at the bodies again before they decomposed any further to see if they might hold more clues that they had missed. The parents agreed and then stood by as their children's graves were disturbed, the bodies removed and transported and searched again. Then, quietly, reverently, the police returned the bodies to their graves.

In March 1956, the police announced to the press that they had found more clues. Metal shavings were found under the fingernails of the boys. Analysis of the shavings indicated that they were a unique alloy that would seem to indicate the boys were murdered in a machine shop somewhere. Again, the police released these details in hopes of getting more tips.

Eventually, the police once again made a plea to the public for information. They held a press conference asking people to essentially spy on their neighbors. They wanted to investigate any suspicious activities and people who had clothing that seemed like that of a young boy in their possession who should not possess such things. This yielded a tip from a maintenance worker who spotted a box of what appeared to be children's clothing in a bedroom. The police were again hopeful because a check of the man who lived in the apartment revealed a history of sex crimes against boys. The man was arrested and questioned for days. However, he did not break and claimed that he had nothing to do with the murders. Eventually, the police were forced to release him, and he also disappeared from the investigation.

The investigation began to grind to a halt. The tips were coming in to law enforcement agencies across the state, but the various departments still did not communicate with one another. Promising leads were kept hidden and clues were not shared. The entire investigation would become the obsession of dozens of investigators, but the investigation itself would prove frustrating beyond words.

The killer or killers seemed to have gone to superhuman lengths to not leave clues. No fingerprints were found. No fibers were found on the body, and no hairs or other elements from the killers were found. The bodies were clean as to their killer's identity, and the crime scene was as well.

When the taskforce to investigate was formed, some of the best detectives in the city were pulled off other cases to focus solely on this one. However, the taskforce was slow to form, and by the time many of these detectives had a chance to see the crime scene, it was weeks after the bodies had been discovered and removed. Meanwhile, other investigators had already trampled all over the area, followed by the press and curiosity seekers. Any valuable evidence that might have been there was long gone.

Ultimately, over the next three years, the police would run down 5,886 different leads. These leads would cause them to interview 43,740 different people. Of those people, 3,270 would undergo intense interrogation. Of those interrogated, the police would make 104 arrests. Of those arrests, 45 people would be indicted. Of the 45 indicted, 40 would be convicted for various crimes, but not the murders. The police would also give 147 different suspects polygraph tests. Polygraphs would also be given to 97 additional people, all of which would lead to nothing. The total number of report pages all of this investigating would lead to totaled six thousand, and all of it led to not a single solid arrest for the murders of Bobby, John and Tony. In the Chicago police, the IBI and the various law enforcement offices of police departments around the Chicago area, the investigation ground to a halt.

Hardened investigators who had put away dozens of criminals for crimes as bad as, if not worse than, the murder of the three boys would be haunted by this case throughout the rest of their careers and into retirement. Many would continue to try and investigate even after they had moved on to other cases. The case sat open in the Chicago Police Department files like an open sore. There is no statute of limitations on murder in Illinois, so the case was still technically under investigation. The days grew into months, which turned into years and then decades. As time wore on, it was thought that the case would never be solved. It seemed as if someone had stepped out of the darkness, brutally murdered three boys and then vanished back into the inky blackness of that night and disappeared forever.

Thus, the case that had shocked the city into locking down their children grew cold. As each year went past, it was felt that the likelihood of catching the killers was becoming less and less. It stayed that way for forty years. However, a name did pop up from time to time in the investigation, even going back to the '50s. It was a name known to some, particularly law enforcement officials in the suburbs. That name was Silas Jayne.

If you look at a map of where the bodies of the three boys were discovered and then check some of the surrounding buildings and businesses, you will notice something. The boys were found in the Robinson Woods Forest Preserve. Roughly one mile away sits Idle Hour Stables.

Silas Jayne was the owner of Idle Hour Stables. Enough of the neighbors who surrounded the stables gave statements to police about noises that they heard coming from that area that police did investigate the stables back in the '50s. What they found was interesting, but not incriminating.

First off, they found resistance. The Jayne family resisted giving the names of employees who worked for the stables. The police sought warrants. A list of employees was eventually turned over, and promises were made that all employees were accounted for on that list. This turned out to be a lie.

In talking to Silas Jayne, the police found a man who, at best, gave them a cold reception. Silas fought them at every turn. People who had never seen or met Silas before discovered how cold his eyes could be and just how intimidating he could be to his employees and even police detectives, and how he could use that to get what he wanted by silencing those who might know anything. When interviews were conducted with employees of the stable, the police were suspicious because so many seemed to be repeating the same statements, as if on autopilot. No one knew anything about anyone or anything, and getting information was worse than trying to pull a tooth from one of the horses in the stables.

Things were growing more and more tense within the Jayne household at the same time that the city was dealing with the tragedy of the three boys. In fact, the shocking story of the blood feud between Silas and his brother George would become intertwined in ways that would lead to speculation for decades. How much either brother knew about what happened to those boys would become a debate that would outlive both men.

At the same time investigators were knocking on Silas's door to ask questions about the employees of Idle Hour Stables, George Jayne was having an argument with his wife. His wife was distraught and upset with him because he had come home claiming he had seen something and knew enough to "put Silas and the rest into the electric chair." His wife pleaded with him to go to the police. Given the fact that Silas had gone from giving dirty looks to his half brother to making outright and very public threats against him, George must have been very tempted to do just that. However, George was a man who had a sense of honor. He may not have been any more educated or couth than his brothers, but he did have some sense of honor. He knew that such a scandal would destroy the Jayne family name. Even more worrying, if Silas found out that he had gone to the police and the police were unable to make the case stick, he and his entire family would be in grave danger. In fact, George was convinced the police were secretly on Silas's payroll and that Silas's reach could extend far beyond prison and still bring about retribution against George and his family.

So while the police were knocking on his door and the door of his brother to find out what was going on, George decided it was best to keep quiet. Exactly what he thought he would do with the information remains unclear. His wife convinced him to write out what he knew in a letter. She would then hide that letter. Some believe that George attempted to use that letter to blackmail his brother. Still others said that it was there as insurance once Silas started to threaten his brother's life. If he were to be killed, it was theorized, that letter would be leaked to the police and the press. Perhaps it was insurance and perhaps it was blackmail, but the letter itself would prove a mystery later on.

In May 1955, a fire was suddenly ignited in the back barn of Idle Hour Stable. It was not said whether any horses died in the fire, but the entire structure was burned to the ground. Investigators found it suspicious and believed that Silas Jayne had deliberately set the fire, but there was no evidence. Silas collected on insurance, and investigators chalked it up to a strange, if very suspicious, coincidence.

When the list of employees at Idle Hour Stables was given to the police, each employee was subsequently questioned. Nothing of importance or use was revealed. Again, there were many investigators who were suspicious that something had happened, but there was no way to prove anything. Frustrated, the interviews were added to the files.

There was one name that was not on that list, however. It would become a very important name years later and prove to be the key to the entire case. That name was Kenneth Hansen, a protégé of Silas Jayne who was so close to the cold-hearted horseman that he called him "Uncle Si."

The man named Kenneth Hansen was born on December 7, 1932. He was the youngest of four to Ethan and Lucille Hansen. He had an older brother and two sisters. There was nothing truly remarkable about his life during much of his youth. His family was not particularly poor, nor were they wealthy. He did not exhibit behavior that friends or family found particularly disturbing.

In 1951, he graduated from Amundson High School. It was then that Kenneth Hansen began to look around for something to do with his life. He was unsure of what he should do and had the decision made for him when he was drafted into the army in 1953. He was assigned to the Fortieth Infantry Division Headquarters Staff.

The Hansen family had enough money to own a few horse stables that were run by Ken as well as his father and his brother. While Ken was serving his time in the army, a man named Herbert Hollatz started boarding at the Park Ridge Riding Academy, the stable owned by the Hansen family. Not long after the young man started working there, the first signs of the darkness lurking within Kenneth Hansen began to manifest themselves. While he was home on leave, he met and sexually assaulted Hollatz. Between 1952 and 1953, this happened several times. At first, Hollatz was a victim, but the sex eventually turned consensual. The two men entered a relationship, something outright scandalous at the time and kept as a secret from anyone, even within Hansen's family.

The idea of being a homosexual was so against the norms of society during the early '50s that Hansen married a woman named Beverly Rae Carlson in June 1953. Their relationship was, at best, rocky for much of their lives. It was Beverly who knew the turmoil inside Hansen as he struggled with his sexuality. She also saw the demons that led him down paths to create even greater and more heinous acts of evil.

In 1954, Silas Jayne bought the Idle Hour Stable, which was located in Park Ridge, not far from the stables owned by Hansen and his family. It is believed that this was when Hansen met Silas, although some say he had met him much earlier. Since both Kenneth and Silas were in the horse business, there was an argument to be made that the two might have met sometime earlier. When Silas bought the Idle Hour, he hired Kenneth Hansen to work for him as a stable hand.

Kenneth was a disturbed man by this point. He was a homosexual who had to completely suppress his urges. Not only were the times he lived in the times when homosexuality was considered a form of insanity, but he also worked in an industry in which homosexuality was not accepted and often met with open hostility. He had fallen into the orbit of a man who lived his life to scam money off of those who were wealthy and had his own predilection for young women. Also, Silas was a man who got what he wanted when he wanted it. Before long, Kenneth Hansen was like Silas's young protégé.

The fateful day came when the murders happened. Kenneth Hansen still worked for Silas at Idle Hour Stables. When the police asked for the list of employees, Kenneth was hidden. When the employees were questioned, Kenneth's name was not mentioned.

Within a week after the murders, Ken Hansen was in bed with Herbert Hollatz. After their afternoon tryst, Kenneth suddenly decided he needed to talk. According to Hollatz, he was asked by Kenneth if he could trust Hollatz. Hollatz, concerned, younger, confused, said yes.

Hansen told Hollatz that he killed the three boys everyone was looking for. Hollatz was, naturally, shocked. However, he was also terrified. He asked Hansen why he did it. He reported that Hansen said, "Someone told me to do it."

Hollatz was now terrified. He stated that Hansen stared at him with his "cold eyes." Hansen then told Hollatz that he had to trust him and if he broke that trust, he would have him killed just like the three boys. Hollatz was now in mortal terror. He was tempted to go to the police, but the threats against him by Hansen had far greater reach to him. He fled.

Before he ran, Hollatz found himself being questioned by police. He said nothing of Hansen. Then he headed west. He never again had a homosexual affair. Instead, he married and settled down. He had children of his own and did his best to forget all about Kenneth Hansen. In fact, he became convinced that Hansen surely had been caught and sent to prison for those murders. To help himself forget Kenneth Hansen, Herbert Hollatz drank—a lot.

Kenneth Hansen seemed untouchable. As the investigation went on around him, the Jaynes seemed to be doing everything they could to keep his name out of police hands. Even George Jayne, fearful of police on his brother's payroll and the damage the scandal may do to the Jayne name, did not reveal to police that Kenneth Hansen worked for Silas. The police did not receive a list of Idle Hour Stables employees until late in October 1955.

Several months later, in 1956, the barn near the back of the lot of Idle Hour Stables burned to the ground. Once again, investigators were suspicious, but there was no mention of a Kenneth Hansen being anywhere near it or having anything to do with operations at the stables.

Kenneth Hansen must have thought he was invincible. He continued his behavior. He routinely had sex with the young stable hands. He also had a habit of driving up and down streets, picking up hitchhikers, bringing them back to the stables and having sex with them. His behavior was tolerated but not accepted by his mentor, Silas Jayne. Silas believed that Hansen's behavior could eventually ruin him. Still, he felt compelled to also cover up the deeds Hansen committed.

In 1958, a stable hand caught Kenneth Hansen having sex in a stable with a young boy. As the two pulled their clothes on, Kenneth threatened the young man. He told him, "If I hear you mention a word to anybody else about this, you'll end up in a forest preserve like some other boys."

Things continued like this for years. In 1962, a young man named Roger Lee Spray was abandoned by his mother and went to live with Ken Hansen and his wife. Beverly Hansen was suspicious of Kenneth, and his behavior was erratic as he continued to hide his sexuality.

Between 1962 and 1963, a man named Edwin Nefeld became friends with Kenneth Hansen. In fact, he bought a horse from the man. Hansen had by that time opened his own stables, called the High Hopes

Stable. The two men eventually met up with Silas Jayne, Frank Jayne Sr. and Frank Jayne Jr. Years later, Nefeld would become police chief of Markham, Illinois. He would also be a kind of hired man for Silas Jayne.

In 1968, a man named William "Red" Wemette was introduced to both Curtis and Kenneth Hansen. Wemette was an informant for the Bureau of Alcohol, Tobacco, Firearms and Explosives (ATF) and other law enforcement agencies. He was being turned toward the show horse and horse industry in the Chicago suburbs, which were suspected of corruption and criminal activity. He was introduced to the Hansen brothers during a card game at the Valley View Young Adults Klub.

Meanwhile, things between Silas Jayne and his brother, George, had deteriorated to the point of violence. In fact, it had become all-out war between the two. Bombs had exploded beneath cars. People had been killed. Silas had machine-gunned a man on his front lawn. He was seen repeatedly making threats against the life of George.

As the '60s came to an end, Silas managed to do what he had threatened for years. George was shot dead in the basement of his own home while celebrating his son's sixteenth birthday. Eventually, the crime was traced back to Silas. As the '70s rolled on, Silas found himself convicted of the murder and sent to prison. The man he had been protecting all those years, Kenneth Hansen, was now on his own.

In November 1970, Chicago Police sergeant John R. Koren wrote out a long report involving the investigation of the murder of George Jayne. He wrote that he believed George was killed because he knew something about the Schuessler-Peterson murders. In fact, it was his hypothesis that George had been blackmailing Silas with information he had hidden away about Silas's involvement in the crimes. The report was filed and read and, years later, widely circulated, but nothing was done with it at the time. There was no hard evidence, and the letter that George was supposed to have written, and that his wife had sworn he wrote, could not be found.

In December 1970, an article was written for the *Chicago Sun-Times* by Art Petacque that backed up Koren's story. He suggested that George Jayne was killed for what he knew. He said that George had evidence hidden away, in addition to his letter, which explained how Silas was involved with the murders. Again, the story was printed, but investigators were hamstrung. They could not go forward with indictments because there was no solid evidence. It was hoped that someone who witnessed something would come forward when the story was printed. Instead, the story vanished, and no new leads came forward. Silas Jayne may have been under investigation, but he still maintained a solid hold on his people. Everyone was terrified to come forward.

In January 1971, Beverly Hansen decided she had had enough. She filed for divorce. She had caught Ken in bed with a stable hand in their home. She hurled threats and then filed the papers. She later changed her mind.

As the investigation of the murder of George Jayne continued, it seemed as if everyone who ever worked for Silas Jayne was questioned. This time, Kenneth Hansen was not spared. He was questioned about what he knew and if he helped pass money to the men who were hired to kill George. He was considered suspicious and arrested. Charges of conspiracy to solicit murder were brought against Kenneth Hansen. However, as the court proceedings moved forward, the charges were dropped for lack of evidence.

The man who questioned Ken Hansen was named Dave Hamm. He could not forget Hansen even as he walked away free. There was something about his demeanor and the way he answered the questions that stuck in Hamm's craw. He thought that Hansen knew something about what happened back in the '50s, but he had nothing that he could prove. Still, he had to stand aside, as in June 1971 Kenneth Hansen walked free of all charges.

In November 1971, Ken Hansen and Beverly reconciled. Ken moved back in with her. However, Kenneth resumed his activities with men, and with young men in particular. He and his brother, Curtis, made threats against any they felt might want to talk about Kenneth and his lifestyle.

Meanwhile, the name of Kenneth Hansen was still in the mind of investigators who were looking into the activities of Silas Jayne. Silas was in prison until the early '80s, serving seven years for conspiracy to commit the murder of his brother. Meanwhile, Silas was now firmly on the radar of many other investigators. His scams were being reviewed. More of his crimes and the crimes of the people he had nurtured and taught were coming to light. Even in prison, his name came up when the heiress to the Brach candy fortune vanished. There was also the matter of a barn being burned down in Wisconsin by Silas's nephew.

As the investigators started looking harder at the life of this man of horses, the name of Kenneth Hansen came up again and again. Investigators all felt that he had been involved in one or more of the crimes, and more importantly, they felt that he might have had something to do with the Schuessler-Peterson murders, still the most notorious unsolved murders in the city's history.

Back in 1972, just before Silas Jayne went on trial for the murder of his brother, a man named Joe Plemmons moved to Chicago. He eventually befriended Kenneth Hansen, which would become important more than two decades later.

Silas Jayne was released from prison after serving for seven years. He stated that he wanted to find the real people behind the murder of his brother. There were others, however, who said that he spent time in prison putting together a "hit list" and wanted to get revenge. He let the suburban newspaper, the *Daily Herald*, interview him. He claimed he was nearly broke from years of fighting in the courts. Meanwhile, the FBI was circling Silas Jayne and his empire in connection with the disappearance of Helen Brach.

Silas Jayne outfoxed them all. He was diagnosed with leukemia. He died quietly in the early '80s, and whatever secrets he may have had died with him. However, the man so many had feared for so long was gone. The floodgates began to open.

On April 14, 1993, three men were sitting down to discuss the case of missing candy heiress Helen Brach. The three men were ATF agent John Rotunno and his supervisor, James Delorto. Also in attendance was former FBI investigator David Hamm.

Helen Brach was into horses. She had owned several throughout her life. She was known to have been associating with a man who bought and sold horses. However, soon after she disappeared, it became evident that the man she was with was another protégé of Silas Jayne. Despite Jayne being in prison, he was suspected of masterminding a scam to bilk Brach out of money and, perhaps, ultimately ordering her removal.

Once the investigators began probing that hornets' nest, they began finding disturbing things. For example, Hamm was the one who arrested

Kenneth Hansen in 1971 and questioned him about his involvement in the murder of George Jayne. He had never been able to forget the man he met and questioned and his possible link to the Schuessler-Peterson murders that had haunted the city and the investigators since the '50s.

As the three men started out talking about the Brach case, the name of Kenneth Hansen came out. Soon, the discussion turned to the case of the three murdered boys. Hansen was mentioned again, this time as a potential suspect.

Silas Jayne was dead by 1993. Those who had been afraid to talk about him may not be as afraid anymore, it was theorized. It might be time to start poking around in some old nests and see what comes out. So, the old case of the murder of three boys was reopened, and the people involved with Idle Hour Stable were questioned again. It took time, tracking down those who had moved to other states, but anyone involved with Silas Jayne or Kenneth Hansen was tracked down, and the questioning resumed.

When the investigators had tried to talk to employees of Idle Hour Stable thirty-plus years ago, they had met with a strange wall of silence. No one wanted to talk about anything, and even getting the full list of employees proved difficult. Now, with the specter of Silas Jayne gone, those who held back were suddenly willing to talk. The cracks in the wall appeared.

In 1995, Herbert Hollatz was back in Chicago watching television. He was watching the local "super station," WGN, and trying to catch up on the day's news. As he watched, he was stricken with fear and dismay. He saw that Kenneth Hansen, his former lover, and the man who threatened him, had been arrested. He learned that, for the past two years, investigators had been piecing together evidence that Hansen murdered Tony, John and Bobby all those years ago.

Hollatz was rocked. His world seemed to tip on its axis. He had been assuming, all of this time, that Hansen was surely arrested for this crime years ago. He had been assuming that Hansen was in prison for the entire time he had been back in the area. Now he found out that none of this had happened. Guilt, fear and shame crashed into him all at once. Hollatz picked up the phone and called one of his daughters. He was emotional and distraught. He had never spoken about his past dalliances with homosexuality. His family was shocked, but his name eventually fell into the hands of prosecutors.

Others who have had relations and relationships with Hansen, sexual or otherwise, were lined up to testify against him. At least three had been told stories, by Hansen, about his involvement in the killings. The stories all differ just slightly, but all of the sources admitted to his doing the killing and Silas Jayne assisting in the cover-up after.

On September 6, 1995, Kenneth Hansen went on trial for the murders of the Schuessler-Peterson boys. Eleanor Schuessler had died in the '80s, never seeing justice done for her two sons. However, the parents of Bobby Peterson both prayed that, at long last, the story of what happened to their son would come out, and the man behind it would pay.

The trial began with a long list of depravity at the hands of Kenneth Hansen. Three men stepped forward to testify about what had Hansen told them happened that fateful day. Evidence of his tendency to pick up hitchhikers was also presented. The trial was not very long, and on September 13, 1995, Kenneth Hansen was convicted of the murders of John and Anton Schuessler and Bobby Peterson.

On October 29, 1995, a judge finally passed sentence against the man convicted of one of the most notorious unsolved murders in the history of Chicago. The courtroom was packed as reporters anxiously awaited the sentence. Hansen was sentenced to two to three hundred years in prison. His health was already questionable at best at the time of the trial, and it was thought that this was a death sentence.

This should have been the end of the story. However, as with many things in our justice system, it was not.

In May 2000, after he had served in prison for five years, Kenneth Hansen's appeals finally reached the Illinois Supreme Court. It was determined by several of the justices that testimony about Hansen's habit, such as the picking up of hitchhikers, was prejudicial and should not have been allowed. They determined, therefore, that the original trial judge, Judge Toomin, erred. They threw out Kenneth Hansen's conviction and ordered a new trial.

So the case that will not go away started over again. In August 2002, Kenneth Hansen, his health failing even further, was put on trial yet again. The evidence was presented again, and witnesses were called, again, to testify. This time, the trial took a bit longer, but Hansen was convicted again.

The Murder of Three Young Boys

On October 1, 2002, the courtroom was packed, yet again, as another judge stepped into the room and passed his sentence. Once more, Kenneth Hansen was sentenced to two to three hundred years for the murders. This time, the charges stuck past his appeals. Kenneth Hansen eventually died in prison in September 2007, putting to rest, once and for all, the case of the three murdered boys.

So, what happened that fateful day? How did those three boys meet their end? What was Kenneth Hansen's involvement, and how did Silas Jayne fit into the story at all?

The problem was that Kenneth Hansen was the one who told the story of what happened. One of his tendencies appears to have been his inability to stop talking about those murders of his male lovers from the time he committed the crime through his imprisonment. His version of the story, however, changed from time to time.

The first person he apparently told was his lover, Herbert Hollatz, a man Kenneth Hansen raped and then convinced to love him. A man who would flee in fear for his life and start over, finding love with a woman and having children, and never engaging in further homosexual behavior. According to Hollatz, Kenneth Hansen had met the boys before. He also told them about his work at the stables and gauged their interest in riding. He made them promises of seeing a new horse at the stable, and on that fateful day, he made plans to pick them up and take them to Idle Hour Stable to ride horses.

According to Hollatz, Hansen picked the boys up as they were hitchhiking on the side of the road and after they had seen the Disney movie. The three boys were excited to see him and excited about spending the evening riding horses at Idle Hour. Hansen took them to the rear-most stable. He told Hollatz he let Peterson ride a horse around the grounds and took John and Anton into a back room. He then proceeded to have sex with both boys.

Hollatz said that Hansen told him Bobby Peterson became curious about what was happening with his two friends and heard sounds coming from the room they were in. He walked in and was shocked. He began yelling at Hansen. He began to threaten Hansen with going to the police. Hansen told Hollatz that he had no choice in the matter.

Hollatz said that he kept an eye on the other two boys, who were now terrified, and blocked their access to a door. He grabbed Bobby Peterson in a chokehold to get him to stop screaming. He told Hollatz he accidentally used too much pressure and killed the boy. This crime, he said, was seen plainly by the other two boys, and he now had no choice but to kill them, too.

At this point, the shouting and commotion had attracted the owner of Idle Hour Stable. Silas Jayne walked into the barn and then into the room to see Hansen standing among the bodies of three young boys. According to Hansen, Silas became infuriated. He began screaming at Hansen and threatening him. "Why do you do this to me?" he reportedly screamed. "Don't you know that this will ruin me?"

Silas calmed down enough to put a plan into action. According to the tale retold by Hollatz, Silas and Kenneth set about trying to cover their tracks. The boys' clothing was removed and destroyed. Jayne and Hansen carried the boys to one of Silas's cars and dumped them in the trunk. They then drove to the forest preserve and removed the bodies, tossing them aside. A few weeks later, when authorities began poking around Idle Hour Stable, Silas had the barn burned down, erasing any evidence that might still have been there.

Another version of the story that Hansen gave differs just slightly. Again, he said he knew the boys and picked them up while hitchhiking. However, in this version it was his fear of being exposed as a homosexual that caused him to turn violent. Hansen said that he murdered the two Schuessler boys first after he finished raping them. Then he had to murder Bobby Peterson, since he was a witness. Again, he said that it was Silas Jayne who helped him dispose of the bodies and, eventually, burned down the barn.

In the third version that Hansen told yet another person, Silas Jayne had a slightly more sinister role. In this version, the boys were brought back, and Hansen had sex with all three. However, Silas Jayne stumbled across the scene and was outraged at what Hansen was doing on his property. He ordered the boys killed, and Hansen obliged. The two then set about covering up the crime.

To this day, some still wonder what role Silas Jayne had in the killings and if it went beyond that which was stated in the trial of Kenneth

Hansen. There has even been a suggestion that Silas may have stumbled across the scene and killed the children himself, or at least killed one or more of them with his hands. Some have stated that Silas's own wife made statements that he told her as much. However, there has never been any solid evidence that Silas had anything to do directly with the murders. As for the cover-up? Well, that much is now part of court record.

However, Silas Jayne would not go to jail for the crimes of the murders of three boys. No, his life was involved in a dispute with his own brother. It was a dispute that would lead to another brutal murder and prove the undoing of Silas Jayne's carefully maintained empire.

CHAPTER 3

BAD BLOOD BETWEEN BROTHERS

The story of Cain and Abel is probably well known to anyone who grew up in the western hemisphere. In the Bible, it says that Cain and Abel were the sons of Adam and Eve. Cain was a farmer, while Abel raised animals. One day, both brothers made offerings to God. Cain's was not found pleasing, but Abel's was. This created such jealousy in Cain that he killed Abel in a rage and hid the body. To punish him, God marked Cain so all would know what he had done.

While the story of Silas and George Jayne is far from biblical, there are certain similarities between the stories. Silas was the oldest brother, but George, in many ways, was the favorite. Silas's father was an abusive drunk, while George's was a lawyer and well respected. Right from the beginning, it seems, Silas had it in for his half brother.

George was given the family name in an attempt to give him legitimacy. Most of the town where his father lived must have known about his true origins. In such a small town, few secrets are really ever hidden. However, George was considered a Jayne and not a Spunner, and if questions were asked, mention of what happened to the asker are not documented.

George, however, was always the favored one, and Silas, never one to let a slight go unpunished, immediately began creating a pool of hatred toward his brother. It was a pool that would grow ever deeper as he grew older and things changed between him and his brother. It was a pool that seemed to have no bottom, and at some point, there seemed to be no length to which Silas would go to kill his own blood. It would become an all-out war between siblings, and unfortunately, innocent bystanders would die along the way. Things may have first gone wrong when Silas was in court trying to defend himself against rape charges at the age of seventeen. As the story goes, he was told by George Spunner that a year in prison would do him some good. Spunner supposedly told the judge the same thing. Spunner and Silas definitely did not get along. Silas was running wild, while Spunner was a lawyer and businessman. He must have looked upon the wild-haired, cold-eyed young man who committed that crime and wondered what would become of him. He stated that he thought a year in prison might scare the boy straight. Instead, that year in prison hardened Silas and helped dig the well of hatred he had for George Jayne a bit deeper.

George was part of the Jesse Jayne Gang that rode in the rodeo and began raising horses. He was incorporated with the rest of the brothers in all of their activities. He was good with horses, as were all of the Jaynes, and an exceptional rider. He was there when the gang gained its reputation of being expert when it came to horseflesh but also as a unit no one wanted to mess with.

There was a story that the brothers had entered a horse competition when Silas was fairly young and George was still in his late teens. It looked like Silas was going to lose the competition. So, while Frank and Silas took turns beating the rider who looked like he was going to win, George held the man's arms. George may have been nicer than his brother, but he was far from a saint.

Compared to his brothers, George grew up refined. There are stories, however, of George attending a cocktail party and whipping off his shoes and socks to pare down his toenails. This goes to show just what his brother's manners were like. They were men who were known for their charm, but they were also known for an air of danger that seemed to surround them.

As the men grew up, all of the brothers went off and opened their own stables. They were all accomplished horse trainers and riders. However,

Frank liked to work closely with Silas. George always seemed to have the desire to spread out on his own, which also bothered Si.

When DeForest Jayne killed himself, he left twenty acres of land near the corners of Waukegan and Caldwell Roads to George. Silas had his own eyes and designs on that land. He considered his brother giving it to the half brother a slap in the face. It was just another reason for him to hate George and dig his well of resentment and hatred deeper.

Silas and George worked together for a long time. However, the deep wounds Silas felt George had inflicted upon him began to fester. Before too long, he would go from burning internally to demonstrative displays of his anger. In 1940, George was dropping by Silas's house for a visit. He got out of his car and began walking up the long walk toward the front door. He may have been able to see Silas as he approached the door, or perhaps Silas was on the front porch. However, as he approached, Silas let one of his beloved Dobermans loose and laughed as it chased George and knocked him down. Silas had done this with others, finding it hilarious, but never with anyone in his own family. George had to beat the dog off with a cane he carried.

Although George was able to ride with the best of them, he was always more of a businessman than his brothers. So when his brothers opened their stables and then began their games of conning wealthy fathers of their money, he didn't readily agree to go along with it. He began looking to open his own stables to train riders and breed horses. The business of horses is a rather strange one. It involves high risk on the part of the horse trader, but the payoffs can be tremendous. A quality horse that wins blue ribbons in competitions can go for thousands upon thousands of dollars. It is a strange mixture of business, sport and hobby. Those who buy horses and those who ride them are often the very rich. The horses are purchased for daughters, mostly, who want their own horses and beg their fathers to buy them. Of course, most self-respecting families want the best horses and are willing to pay top dollar for them. Then the stable owners get to make money to train the riders as well as to keep and take care of the horses. Those with talent in this business stood to make a lot of money, and the Jayne brothers were all good when it came to horses.

Silas, however, liked to intimidate people. He often invented crimes to fit the profile he wanted to create for himself. For example, he liked to tell the story of how he spent a year in Joliet Penitentiary for stabbing a man. He used to describe, in detail, how it felt to stab the man and watch the blood ooze from the wound. It was an impressive story, to be sure, but it was entirely fabricated. He had spent a year in jail for rape, but he had not murdered anyone at that point.

George began setting up his own stables in the '40s. Even then, however, he was still in relatively good graces with his brother Silas. In fact, his brother loaned him money and helped him set up his first stables. They were still working together in many horse shows and competitions into the 1950s. They shared the winnings, and it was a time of relative peace between them. Sadly, it would not last.

Some within the family would say that their first disagreements came over American Horse Shows Association rules. Silas simply did not believe in many of the rules and would flaunt or outright ignore them. George, meanwhile, was a believer and did want to follow them. Arguments erupted. Silas also did not believe in playing fairly. He tried to get George to go along with him in intimidating competitors at horse shows. Silas was elevating the kinds of things he wanted to do from just beating up a competitor while George held the man's arms. Silas wanted to bomb their homes and stables. Silas once told George to break the leg of a healthy horse, and George outright refused. Silas went into a rage.

Silas did not play fair anywhere. He would often use anesthetic injected into the joints and legs of horses nearly crippled with arthritis. He would then show off these horses to the rich parents looking to buy their little girl a prize and present papers from veterinarians verifying the health of the horse. Silas once approached a vet named Dr. Thomas Phillips with such a deal. He wanted Phillips to certify the health of a horse with severe arthritis and then promised the doctor a generous share of the sale. Phillips refused, and Silas threatened him. Still he refused. Then, one day, a bomb exploded near Phillips's clinic. A few moments later, he got a phone call saying that the next one would be at his home. Soon after, he signed the papers.

Another time, in 1961, a man tried to sue Silas for selling him a lame horse. He brought the lawsuit to court, and proceedings were set to commence. However, a bomb exploded just outside the man's house, causing extensive damage. Soon after, he dropped the lawsuit.

Silas and George Jayne were still on common enough ground for Silas to loan George $90,000. George used it to buy Happy Day Stables at the intersection of Cumberland and Montrose. The brothers used the stables together for some time. It was yet another era of some peace between the two. Silas would eventually move his operations over to Idle Hour Stable and start training riders and competing against George. It was now 1954, and the truce was soon to be over.

George's home caught fire and burned down completely not long after Silas started his own operation. Silas was angry because he wanted George to buy his home and stable and George had refused. George always blamed Silas for the fire, but there was no proof. George stated to his family that he still hoped he and Si could maintain some kind of brotherly relationship despite competing with each other. The rivalry was intense but still was somewhat civil until 1961. Then things went from a kind of cold war into a very hot war.

In May 1961, Silas was attacked at his home. Gunmen opened fire on the house, and Silas attacked back, engaging in a gun battle. The police arrived at Silas's home, and he fingered four mob-connected men with the attack. The police found the four men hiding out in Wisconsin, and they were arrested. However, it soon became evident to investigators that the four men had nothing to do with the shooting. Exactly why Silas sent law enforcement on such a wild goose chase was never made clear. Whether the four men had anything to do with George is also not clear, but Silas was suddenly on edge and more likely to get violent than ever before.

George and Silas were showing up at the same horse shows now. George's fourteen-year-old daughter was his main rider at this point. She had talent, and George was getting great horses. George was starting to win, and this was probably the greatest sin that Silas could imagine being committed against him. In the middle of 1961, George's daughter won the top prize at the Oak Brook Hounds Horse Show and beat Silas's top rider. Silas was enraged. He was not the type of person who kept his anger to himself. He was not afraid to yell and scream and make his threats in public. So after the show, in front of other riders, an audience and George's daughter, Silas tracked George down and began screaming at him. "I'll never talk to you gain!" he screamed.

Not long after, another incident happened that was like a slap in Silas's face. Silas had a young rider named Cheryl Lynn Rude riding for him. She had tremendous talent but was barely eighteen years old. However, according to Rude, Silas demanded sex from her, and she refused. According to Silas, she wasn't a very good rider, and he fired her. Regardless of which version of the story is true, Rude left Silas's stables and began looking for someone else to ride for. George Jayne knew talent when he saw it, and he stepped in and offered her a chance to ride for him. She accepted.

To Silas, this was the greatest insult George could have possibly committed against him. He burned with fury. It was then, many believe, that he first decided he was going to have to kill George. Things only got worse as the competitions continued.

George now had two riders who were both capable of winning competitions and beating Si. George's daughter was still riding, and now Cheryl Rude was also winning blue ribbons around the country. Silas's horses were having a steady streak of losing, and it was not sitting well with him.

Throughout the country, at competition after competition, Silas yelled at George. In addition to threatening to never speak to him again, he also made threats against his life. George and his men started carrying guns, and George hired bodyguards.

Still, in 1961, Cheryl Rude won the Oak Brook Horse Show. Silas protested, claiming she had missed a jump. His protest was denied, and she claimed first place. Silas tracked George down and, once again in front of witnesses, screamed, "You SOB! I'll kill you!"

This went on for several years. In 1963, at the Northwestern Horse Show, just before the junior championship, George decided to talk to Silas. George's daughter was in competition for a ribbon, and he was worried about what Silas might say or do. He found Silas and told him, "Don't bug my daughter." Silas screamed back, "Shut up or I'll kill you!"

In 1964, at the Lake Forest Horse Show, George's daughter rode again. It looked like she was going to win and take another prize away from her Uncle Silas. She was atop her horse, getting ready to enter the ring, when she heard voices. Her father and her uncle were arguing. Although she could not hear everything over the din of the crowd and other noises, she clearly heard her Uncle Silas scream, "I'll kill you!"

After that, the threats kicked into high gear. George began switching the places where he ate dinner, never repeating the same restaurant two nights in a row. He and all of his entourage were armed at all times, particularly during horse shows. None of this seemed to stop Silas. He was moving forward with plans to kill his brother and seemed to take great delight in torturing him by threatening George at every turn.

Later in 1964, Silas tracked George down at the International Amphitheater during a horse show. Glaring, his cold eyes filled with menace, he told George, "I'll get you, one way or another."

Not long after, while attending a show in Kansas City, George found himself alone again. He was standing on the ramp up one of his trailers when Silas suddenly appeared in his Cadillac. Silas drove his car up the ramp, pushing George up against the trailer. Silas told George, "You'll never make it home."

George had been telling people for a while that he felt that Silas had it in for him. He had told Cheryl Rude's family that he thought Silas wanted to do him in. He began writing letters that were to be delivered to key people in his life if he were to meet a suspicious end. These letters were hidden away, to be released only after George's death. George made it out of Kansas City, but he had time to look back at all of the evidence that seemed to show that Silas was out to get him any way he could.

In 1962, George's office was burglarized. Files were stolen, along with key accounting information. In March 1963, George's office, clubroom and stables were riddled with bullets. Investigators found over twenty bullets in the walls of his office. Sugar was poured into George's gas tank, and his men reported having to dodge sniper fire while going through their workday. At one time, two of George's prized horses were poisoned. In May 1964, George's tackroom at the Cincinnati Horse Show was set on fire.

Things were building. Little did George know that Silas was attempting his first potentially lethal move. Silas did not want to do his own dirty work at this time, so he set some of his men on it. The final straw that would send Silas forward with his plan of action was about to happen in May 1965. The incident need almost not have occurred. In late 1964, Cheryl Rude was injured while riding on George's property. She landed so hard that she ended up in the hospital in critical condition for twelve days. However, Rude was strong and determined. She was one of the best riders George had ever had, and she fought back. By May 1965, she was riding again. In fact, she was riding so well that she, once again, soundly defeated Silas's horse in a show. She witnessed Silas threaten George.

In June, Silas gave the go-ahead for his men to enact his plan to kill George. He used code words, but they knew what it meant, and a man named James Blottiaux headed for the South Side of Chicago. He purchased twenty-one sticks of dynamite from a construction supply company. He stated that he worked for Genson Construction, which was a company that did not exist. He also ordered blasting caps and more cases of dynamite that he indicated he would pick up at another time. He never picked up the rest of the dynamite.

Silas would have preferred to see George shot down like an animal. However, George was constantly surrounded by bodyguards. When George appeared at a horse show and had to make an appearance in the ring or in public, he made sure that there were horses on all sides of him. He hoped that, if there were any snipers in the arena, the horses would provide some cover.

It was early in June 1965 when the first lethal volley was fired. George had met with Cheryl Rude, and they discussed the upcoming shows and the new horses that George had in his stable. In fact, he had some new horses that he wanted to show Cheryl that very morning. Once they had met at George's house, they made their way through the sunlit yard toward the barn.

George was a little like his brother in that he loved Cadillacs. While George was a little more refined than his brother, he also liked to make a splash with his vehicle. Glinting in the morning sun, blocking the large doors of the barn, was George's gold Cadillac.

George made his way around the side of the barn. He intended to go inside and open the barn doors. As he walked away, he smiled and tossed his keys to the beautiful young woman who had won him so much and been one of the best things his stable had ever brought on board. George had to make a phone call and intended to use a phone inside the stable. He asked Cheryl if she would be willing to move his car, perhaps closer to the house, while George opened the barn.

As George headed inside the barn, Cheryl Lynn Rude, in her early twenties and a riding champion, strode calmly over to George's car. She unlocked the door and climbed into the driver's seat. In the morning sunlight, she started the car and then shifted into reverse. Just then, the sticks of dynamite strapped to the bottom of the car exploded. The explosion was terrific. Cheryl was likely killed instantly. The front of the Cadillac was blown apart. George was knocked off his feet as he neared the side door of the barn. The Cadillac was immediately engulfed in flames. Cheryl Rude never stood a chance.

Silas was furious. "We missed him," he reportedly told his men. He was now more determined than ever to get George. However, he also needed to try to cover himself for the death that had just happened at his command. Loose ends had to be tied up.

Investigators were brought in, and the feud that had been brewing in relative privacy amidst the Jayne family was now very public. Police officers immediately noticed the difference between the two brothers. Silas was the charmer, capable of talking his way out of anything, even among cops, but he was cold and ruthless. With Silas, there was an air of menace. With George, there was not that air of menace. George was all about business. George told investigators he was sure it was Silas who had arranged for the bomb to be planted and that he was the intended target. The feud between the brothers now became the focus of the investigation of the death of Cheryl Rude.

James Blottiaux became the focus of the investigation almost immediately. The records showing that he had bought the dynamite were found. Witnesses were lined up against him. However, suddenly, the evidence against him disappeared. Even though Blottiaux was arrested, the charges against him were dropped. Investigators were all but sure that it was Blottiaux who planted the actual bomb, but now the evidence was gone.

The death certificate for Cheryl Rude was finally filled out, and it stated that she was killed by person or persons unknown. Meanwhile, Silas stepped up his determination to kill George. He had already approached more people and asked them if they would like to accept money to kill his brother.

Renee Bruhl was all of nineteen years old in 1966. She was married, and there were some rumors, mostly among her family, that there might have been some tension between her and her husband. None of this was ever proven, but it would be forced into the light during the month of July 1966. That was the year Renee and two of her friends simply vanished, never to be seen again.

The two friends were Patty Blough, nineteen, and Ann Miller, twenty-one. The three women had known one another for some time. All three women were from fairly well-off families, and all three of them were horse enthusiasts. Bruhl even owned a thoroughbred named Hank that she liked to ride on weekends. All three women were known to ride regularly at Tri Color Stables in Palatine, Illinois, which was owned by George Jayne.

July 2, 1966, was bright and gorgeous. Despite what most people think, Chicago does get warm during the summer months. When that happens, the citizens of the great city flock to lakes scattered across the state. Those in and around Chicago are particularly fond of Lake Michigan. The city is lined with beaches that are packed during the particularly hot months of July and August. During that time of year, it is not uncommon for the air temperatures to reach into the eighties and nineties and even past three digits. With the humidity that is common in the Midwest, those heat indexes climb even higher.

While there are beaches right near downtown Chicago, there are other areas that are just as popular. One area is just across the border in Indiana. These are known as the Indiana Dunes, and it is a state park, with jurisdiction over what happens there falling to the park rangers. The dunes are a series of rolling sand dunes all leading down to beaches and the cool Lake Michigan waters. Every year, these beaches become packed with sunbathers, swimmers and boaters. The community around the dunes also builds every summer, becoming like a summer resort town.

Patty, Ann and Renee had plans to head to the Indiana Dunes on that bright, sunny, hot July 2. They planned to leave early that morning and spend the entire day bathing in the sun and maybe swimming in the lake.

Ann Miller had the car and, thus, was given the driving duties. She drove to Blough's home in Westchester, Illinois, and picked her up at 8:00 a.m. There she spoke to Blough's family, and both women stated that they planned on being back sometime in the early evening.

They made one more stop, picking up Renee Bruhl. The three young ladies were seen at a local drugstore soon after. They all bought suntan lotion and appeared to be having a good time. They seemed to be average young women out to have a good time at the beach. Witnesses at the crowded beach would later tell investigators that they saw the women arrive at about 10:00 a.m.

The beaches were packed that day. The three young women cut a very striking vision as they crossed the sand. All three were young, tanned and beautiful. They were all dressed in their best bathing suits, which were more for showing off than for swimming. Several witnesses saw them stroll across the sand and find a spot not far from the water. Witnesses would say that the three women set up their spread about one hundred yards from the water's edge. The three set up blankets and towels, settled on their respective blankets or towels and began applying suntan lotion.

They had quite a spread on the beach. They had radios, robes, wallets and blankets. They all wore sunglasses. In short, they were memorable to the couples, families and single men who were also enjoying the warm sun and the cool waters.

The waters were jammed with boats as well. Pleasure boats of all sizes and shapes crisscrossed the waters not far from shore. There were also various inlets and piers where boaters could keep their boats and then lead them out into the potentially rough waters of Lake Michigan.

Witnesses reported that all three women stood up, as one, and left their spot on the beach about noon. Those who were near their beach spread never saw them again. However, there were so many other witnesses about their previous activities that were definitely seen and their activities were noted.

In the days after the three women vanished, witnesses from all over the dunes would come forward. They said they saw three women who matched their description talking to an unidentified man who was driving a fourteen- to sixteen-foot-long white boat with a blue interior. Meanwhile, about one hundred yards from the beach, the women left all of their belongings, from towels and robes to sunglasses. Witnesses on the beach did not see the three women again.

As the day wore on, those who had seen the three women noticed that they had not returned. They knew that these women were unlikely to have left clothing and radios behind on the beach. One couple finally raised an alarm with the park rangers and expressed their concern over the fact that the young women had not returned as the day wore on. The rangers took note. They also walked to where the blankets and belongings were and gathered the things together. They stored them in a park ranger station for when, they assumed, the women would eventually come back looking for them.

The families of the three women, as might have been expected, were starting to panic. On July 4, Blough's father contacted the park rangers. He told them that his daughter had spent the day at the dunes on July 2 and never returned. He then contacted the police and officially filed a missing persons report. The rangers started a more official investigation at that point. They wandered into the parking lot and found Miller's car. They searched the car but found no indication the girls had ever returned to it after they had parked it there the morning of July 2. They then searched the belongings they had stored and found Miller's keys among her abandoned belongings. The rangers reported what they had found, or not found, to the local police. They then alerted the Coast Guard, since the girls may have vanished while on the lake.

On July 5, 1966, the official search for the three women began. Volunteers and law enforcement officials, including members of the Coast Guard and the park rangers, began a systematic search of the sand dunes. More volunteers and members of the Coast Guard began searching the waterways around the dunes that lead in and out of Lake Michigan.

Before too long, the search was expanded. It soon included a six-mile stretch of beach just west of the Indiana Dunes. That beach was more public than the dunes, and the searchers began putting out information in the press. Before too long, the public contacted local law enforcement and began giving conflicting stories of what had been seen that fateful day. Many of the witnesses gave differing statements about where they had seen the girls. Some of them substantiated each other. The most consistent statement was that the three women were seen around a white boat with blue interior. The description of the man in the boat was that of a man in his mid-twenties. He was described as tanned with dark, wavy hair. He was seen wearing a beach jacket.

One of the witnesses from that day stepped forward and said that he had been filming with a home movie camera at the beach that day. He was certain he had caught the three women at some point during their stay at the dunes. He offered the films to law enforcement. Investigators took up the offer and began reviewing the films. They turned up some interesting images.

The witness with the camera had filmed a lot at the beach that day. There was also a lot of footage of the boats in the area at that time. Before long, investigators had narrowed their interest down to two boats. The first was a sixteen- to eighteen-foot trimaran runabout. The man who owned the boat fit the description the reliable witnesses had given investigators of the man seen speaking to the women from the boat. The second boat was a twenty-six- to twenty-eight-foot-long Trojan cabin cruiser with three men aboard. They had also, at one point, been seen in the company of three women who might have matched the description of Bruhl, Miller and Blough.

As the investigators reviewed the footage, they became very sure that the footage showed the three women on the smaller of the two boats during at least one sweeping shot of the boats from the shore. Investigators went back to witness statements and tried to match what the film showed.

Witnesses claimed to have seen the three women on the cabin cruiser sailing around the beach area just off the dunes. Some more witnesses said they saw the women get dropped off at the beach at about 3:00 p.m. The cabin cruiser went off to pick up more male friends, and they had scheduled a time to pick the girls up again later. The three women were reported walking along the sand dunes right about 3:00 p.m. More witnesses reported that they saw the women approached by another man not long after and that all of them climbed into another boat and went out to the cabin cruiser. Other elements were reported, but these events were corroborated and were considered the most reliable.

Investigators were stumped. They began talking to family members and investigating the personal lives of the three women. This is when they found out that Blough had reportedly been having some marital problems. However, when they questioned her family about these reports, they denied that it was true.

One report from friends of Blough stated that earlier in the year, she had shown up at an event with a facial injury. Her friends thought that the wound looked like it could have been about the same size as a fist. When they asked her about it, she reported that she had been having some problems with the "horse syndicate people."

All three women were known to ride horses. All three had ridden horses and taken lessons at George Jayne's Tri Color Stables in Palatine, Illinois. As the investigators began looking into their personal lives, they found themselves crossing paths with the infamous feud between the two Jayne brothers. Investigators knew that Cheryl Rude had just been killed in an apparent attempt to kill George Jayne. The question became, did the three women see something that could have made Silas Jayne and his crew want to eliminate them? Perhaps the three women had seen someone planting the dynamite that had killed Cheryl Rude.

Investigators questioned Silas and George. George had known the women, but he had no information on what they had seen. Silas, meanwhile, would brag that he had three bodies buried beneath his house. So confident was Si that he could intimidate and buy off witnesses and the police that he felt confident enough to "joke" with police about the supposed bodies he had buried beneath his house.

Silas dodged another investigative bullet. The sheriff took his joke seriously. He began the process of getting a warrant to search Silas's property. However, the sheriff died in a farming accident on his property before the warrant proceedings could commence. The warrants were soon forgotten, and the lead was dropped.

Over the years, there have been supposed sightings of the three women, but none of them has ever turned up anything. The leads have long since grown cold, and the bodies of the three women have never been recovered.

Did they die because they saw something at Tri Color Stables? No one knows for sure and probably never will. However, investigators seem pretty sure that they were more collateral damage of the feud between George and Silas Jayne. They were more damage just for Silas's desire for more power, more wealth and, most of all, to kill his brother.

The Jayne farmhouse in Elgin, Illinois, today.

The farmhouse where Silas Jayne lived until his death.

The field on Our Day Farm in Elgin, Illinois.

Our Day Farm was Silas Jayne's final residence, at 10 North 112 Nelser Road in Elgin, Illinois.

Our Day Farm pasture in Elgin, Illinois.

The former location of Idle Hour Stables in Park Ridge, Illinois.

The bodies of the Schuessler and Peterson boys were recovered near the entrance to the Robinson Woods Forest Preserve.

The entrance to the Robinson Woods Forest Preserve today. In October 1955, brothers Anton and John Schuessler and Bobby Peterson were murdered after being lured to Idle Hour Stables and then left here.

Robinson Woods Forest Preserve near the Des Plaines River in Illinois.

Jayne on his farm in Elgin in 1979. *Courtesy of Paddock Publications.*

Silas Jayne at home with his third wife, Dorothy, in 1979. *Images on this page courtesy of Paddock Publications.*

Silas Jayne with his lawyers in June 1971, when he was on trial for conspiring to kill his brother George Jayne.

Jayne telling his story to the *Sunday Herald* in June 1979.

Jayne on his farm in 1979.

George Jayne was a paranoid man now. He began changing the restaurants he ate at with more frequency. When he started his car, he started it with his feet on the ground and outside the car so that an explosion would, in theory, blow him away from the vehicle instead of burning him inside it.

Shortly after the explosion that killed Cheryl Rude, two men approached George. Their names were Steve Grod and Edward Moran. They told George that Silas had hired them to kill him. However, they both liked George and wanted to turn against Silas. They urged George to hire his own hit man and strike Silas first. George refused. He urged the men to go to the police.

The police took what the two men had to say seriously. However, they wanted solid evidence of Silas making threats against his brother's life. They convinced Grod to have another meeting with Silas and to wear a wire. Grod met with Silas at a horse show in Wisconsin and got him talking. During the course of the conversation, Silas told Grod that it was "time to buy a horse." Grod explained that this was code for "time to try and kill George." Silas gave Grod a down payment of $1,000 for the hit. The authorities thought they were finally going to get Silas Jayne and indicted him for conspiracy to commit murder.

Prosecutors were excited to present their star witness. They thought they had the man who had conspired to kill Cheryl Rude and who had intended to kill his brother. Other investigators were sure they had the man who was responsible for the disappearance and death of three young women. Silas sat with his customary cold stare and glared at the jury as the evidence was presented against him. He bore cold steel through Grod when the man entered the courtroom and took the stand, was sworn in and sat down to give his testimony. What he said shocked prosecutors.

"I can't even remember what I had for breakfast this morning," he replied when asked to relate the conversations that had taken place between him and Silas Jayne. "I'm sick."

Their star witness suddenly couldn't remember anything that had transpired between him and Silas. Grod was indicted for contempt of court and spent time in jail. The case against Silas Jayne fell apart, and the charges were dropped. Once again, with a cold glare saved for his hated brother, Silas Jayne walked out free as a bird. It is believed he paid off Grod generously for his "amnesia."

Of course, George Jayne, being from the family that he was from, was not a saint. Although murder did not seem to be in him, he was not above running scams to get money. However, because he was close to his family and seemed unable to keep secrets from his brother, Silas did make attempts to ruin his brother financially as well as trying to kill him.

At one time, a man named Patrick Butler came to George with an interest in buying a horse. Butler was already well known among the brothers as a buyer of quality horses. George began telling him about a horse named Happy Landings and raved about how great the horse was. Butler considered George an honest man, and George raved about the horse so much that he was almost willing to buy the horse sight unseen. Butler did see the horse before he purchased it. It seemed fine, and he paid $18,000 for Happy Landings. Landings even won a blue ribbon for Butler. However, no sooner did that happen than Happy Landings began showing that he was not the quality horse that George had led Butler to believe he was. The horse began limping and was unable to compete. Silas stepped in, took Butler aside and told him that Happy Landings had arthritis and had been grossly overvalued. In fact, Happy Landings was worth maybe $8,000, and George had pocketed the extra $10,000 he had charged for the horse.

It turned out that George had taken at least one page out of his· brother's book. He had used anesthetic to ease the horse's pain in its painfully arthritic legs. Butler stated he also believed that George bribed the judges to win the one blue ribbon Happy Landings was able to provide to Butler. Butler then checked with Happy Landings's Canadian owner and discovered that Silas was right: George had conned him.

George could have been ruined, but he was able to spread money around and get himself out of trouble. He may not have been a saint, but he did not plan to kill anyone. He even refused to hire a hit man to go after the man who was trying to kill him. George continued to hope that he could find a peaceful solution to the feud between him and Silas. He began searching for further solutions, and at least one led to disaster and another collateral death.

Before he took that step, he tried to sue for peace on his own at least one more time. In early 1967, the entire Jayne family made an attempt to quell the feud. A family reunion was scheduled, with the entire point being to bring George and Silas to the bargaining table to come to terms that would cease the ever-increasing violence. Silas and George did meet, and they did adjourn to a room by themselves. According to Silas, he asked George to stop running scams to sell broken-down horses. He stated that George doing so was bringing shame to the Jayne family. This is how Silas operated. Although it has since been established that Silas did that as much, if not more, than George, he denied it up until his death.

According to statements George made, Silas was really upset over the fact that his horses and Silas's were competing directly with one another. Silas wanted George to stop competing. George claimed that he agreed to stop competing against Silas. According to both men, they shook hands and agreed to peaceful terms. Later on, Silas would claim that the feud, as far as he was concerned, ended in 1967.

Not long after the peace accord, George's daughters got married, one right after the other. According to statements made by the Jayne family, George paid Silas a large sum of money at both weddings in return for the promise that Silas would not do anything to disrupt the weddings. Again, the family said that Silas and George agreed and peace was obtained.

However, George was still paranoid. He knew that Silas was not one to just agree to settle differences. He knew that Silas was not the type of person to just forgive and forget. So George took steps to ensure that he would, at the very least, have advance warning if Silas was headed toward his home. George also wanted additional protection and someone to monitor the activities of his brother. This decision would prove to be the final blow to whatever hopes the Jayne family had for peace between the two.

George hired a man named Frank Michelle Sr. It was 1969, and someone had just lobbed a stick of dynamite at George's home. The damage was, luckily, minimal, but it signaled to George that the peace accord was about to be broken. Michelle was a former police officer, and he was now a private investigator and bodyguard.

Michelle had an idea of tracking Silas. He arranged for a tracking device to be attached to the bottom of Silas's Cadillac. He gave George the receiver, which would beep whenever Silas was within a certain proximity to him. For months, the transmitter worked perfectly, and George was able to do whatever he needed to whenever his receiver would start to beep to ensure that his family was safe. However, after a few months, the transponder stopped working. Michelle figured that the batteries had worn out.

Frank Michelle Sr. recruited his own son, Frank Jr., to help. He gave his son a replacement transponder, directions to Silas's home and the tools he would need to find the transponder and make the replacement. Frank Michelle Jr. was given a ride to Silas's house by his wife, with his young son in the car as well. Michelle climbed out of the car and vanished into the darkness.

Depending on who was spoken with, there were at least two different stories as to what happened that night. In addition, Silas's version changed and was embellished over the course of years. Silas's version was, as one might expect, vastly different from the story that authorities came to believe and put Silas in the victim role.

According to Si, he was sitting at his home watching television. Apparently, according to Si, it was not unusual for him to be sitting in the living room and watching television with several different firearms around him. He claimed that, suddenly, he heard his dogs barking, and then shots rang out. Bullets ripped through his front door. Silas took his pistol and fired back. He later claimed that he heard the shooter cry out when one of his bullets hit the man. Not feeling he had done enough, Silas then grabbed a carbine rifle and stepped out onto his porch. He would tell authorities he saw the gunman crawling across his lawn, heading for a fence, trying to get away. Silas emptied the rifle into the middle of the man, killing him.

As the years went by, the story changed. As he neared the date of his death, Silas told a reporter that the initial volley of gunfire wounded him. He claimed there was a knock on the door, and as he neared the door, the gunfire erupted. He stated that a bullet passed through his abdomen but he still returned fire.

Silas told this story to police. Whether he paid police is up for debate, but authorities in later years would state that they believed he did pay off authorities. He was not prosecuted, and it was labeled a case of self-defense. Of course, Silas would later brag that he had gotten away with murder by paying off the police.

The ATF had a different story about what happened that night. Agents would later admit this to Frank Michelle Sr. after Silas was no longer considered a threat. Their version of the story indicated that Michelle did creep onto Silas's property in the dark of night. However, Silas's dogs were alerted when he made too much noise. According to agents, Silas sicced his dogs on the intruder, and Michelle was brought down by the Dobermans.

Agents would later state that Silas walked calmly into the night, gun in hand, and found Michelle trying to defend himself against the dogs. They claimed that Silas called off the dogs and had Michelle dragged into a private area, where he proceeded to torture the man. Agents stated that Silas used pliers with a locking grip to crush Michelle's testicles until he told Silas who had hired him and why. When he had the information he wanted, Silas shot Michelle.

Once Silas heard that his brother was behind the intruder and what he had been doing, the peace accord was off. There was no turning back Silas from what had been his mission for so long. From that moment on, as far as Silas Jayne was concerned, his brother George was a dead man. However, Silas did not want to do the killing himself, as much as he admitted that he desired to kill George with his bare hands, so he had to turn to his men, find the right ones and have them kill George.

Edwin Nefeld was a cop from Markham, Illinois. Markham had a reputation for having some of the most corrupt police in the state of Illinois, and Nefeld was right at the top of the ladder. He had been on Silas's payroll for some time, providing him with muscle. Nefeld acted as an enforcer and did much of Silas's dirty work. Silas had to merely give the order, and it was up to Nefeld to see those orders carried out. Silas turned to him again in order to have George eliminated once and for all.

Nefeld began searching for a man to do the job. He knew a man named Melvin Adams and decided he might be just the right man. Adams was a wild young man at that time and had had several run-ins with the law. He had pulled a gun on at least one man but had never killed anyone. However, as a man seemingly at war with the world, he was willing to at least consider doing a murder-for-hire.

Nefeld approached Adams and asked if he was interested. Adams said he was. The money was good, more than anything Adams was making in his current job, and he was just wild enough to consider the opportunity exciting. Nefeld arranged a meeting between Silas and Adams. On the night they met, Silas was in a great mood. Adams would later state that Silas was positively giddy, unable to sit still, now that he had someone willing to kill George. Silas agreed to pay Adams $20,000 for the job and then he gave Adams suggestions on how to do it.

Silas first told Adams that he had been trying to kill George for ten years. He stated that Adams might want to consider machine-gunning him on the highway as he drove to work. He also suggested that a bomb might work. He told Adams that it would be wise not to leave any witnesses when he did the crime. He coldly stated that if he killed George at his home and George's wife and children were there, Adams should kill them as well.

Silas told Adams that he had "everything he would need. Lawyers, money, anything."

Adams began setting about his task. However, once he started, he discovered that he didn't quite have the stomach for murder that he thought he had. Despite being wild and willing to accept any job, the idea of walking up to a man and killing him soon proved challenging to Adams.

He later told authorities that he began following George all over the country. While George was attending a horse show in New Orleans, he had no idea that Adams was there, following his every move. At one point, Adams was only a few feet behind George, his hand in his pocket on the gun he was carrying. However, he found himself unable to pull the trigger.

At another point, Adams decided that he was going to kill George in his own home. He drove out to George's home and walked toward the front door. He still held the gun in his hand and was determined to gun George down in his own doorway. Instead, he stood on the front porch, unable to even knock, let alone shoot George down.

Silas was getting impatient. He summoned Adams to his home and asked for a report and, more importantly, an explanation as to why, after months, George was not dead yet. Adams feared for his own life at this point. He told Silas that George was simply too hard to pin down and that he had been unable to find George alone so he could do the job. Silas bought the excuse, and he upped the ante. He increased the amount that he was willing to pay Adams to $30,000. He suggested that Adams might want to find someone to help him. In fact, he suggested that Adams might want to pay someone else to kill George altogether. So Adams turned to one of his co-workers, a man named Julius Barnes.

Unlike Adams, Julius Barnes had no reservations about accepting $10,000 and killing another human being. The two men began shadowing George around, and finally, on October 28, 1970, the two men decided it was time to do the job for which they had been paid.

They drove out to Inverness, the very exclusive suburb where George Jayne and his family had their home. Barnes had a rifle in his lap. Adams was the driver and lookout. They parked near George's home, and Barnes got out of the car. As Adams looked around, watching for any neighbors or police, Barnes crept his way across George's front lawn and then crawled around the corner of George's house.

Inside George's home, there was a celebration going on. George's son was turning sixteen years old, and his family was having a small dinner and party for him. The dinner had just finished, and now the family was going to play bridge in the basement. George shuffled the cards, and he and his son decided they would be on the same team. They made jokes about the women beating them. His daughter sat on one side and his son on the other. Across from George was his wife, Marion.

Outside, Julius Barnes had situated himself on his stomach and viewed the scene of domestic bliss and celebration with growing annoyance. George was facing the basement window, but his wife kept getting in the way of Barnes's shot. He was slightly higher, aiming at a slanted angle through the window. The rifle was cradled in his arms, the butt against his shoulder, his eyes coldly peering down the sight. He waited as the wind blew and Adams watched nervously inside the still running car. Then, just as he was about to give up in frustration, Marion went into the kitchen. Julius Barnes took his shot.

He fired only one bullet. George suddenly stopped moving, letting out a single scream, and then he fell to the floor. The window was shattered, and the bullet traveled at a downward angle. It caught

George in the chest and exited from his lower back. He fell to the floor as his children screamed and his wife ran back into the basement room. Marion ran to George's side. George was still alive, his breathing labored. His children ran to the phone and called for an ambulance. As Marion cradled George in her arms, his blood pouring through her fingers, staining his clothing and covering the floor, George Jayne died from the single gunshot wound. The bullet had nicked his heart, and he didn't stand a chance. Silas had won the feud, but it would prove to be his undoing.

Marion contacted her friends and family even before many of them had heard that George was dead. Immediately, everyone blamed Silas for the murder, and many of George's friends and co-workers wanted to get revenge immediately. Marion told them to hold off seeking revenge. She wanted to do things legally, if possible. By the end of the day George was murdered, Marion gave a press conference at the end of her driveway, in front of George's home. She offered a monetary reward for any information about George's murder.

The letters George had written and that were to be distributed upon his death began to surface with their addressees. Each letter, although each was written slightly differently, blamed Silas for his death should his death be suspicious. He had sent one letter, dated July 16, 1969, to his lawyer. Inside that letter, it stated: "I know without a doubt that he plans to kill me and someday will probably be successful. To date I've been lucky for he persists in hiring only amateurs that he can control and are frightened of him."

Of course, the police zeroed in on Silas as well. However, Silas was so confident that he could bribe, threaten or charm his way out of anything that he showed no fear. It was as if he was daring the police to come and get him. He was already blaming George's "questionable" business practices as the reason he was killed.

Despite Adams's best efforts to be a successful lookout, there were witnesses to the events on that day. A boy who was riding a bicycle in Inverness on the day George was shot provided a description of a car parked in front of George's home. He even had a partial license plate number. The description of the car and the partial plate was enough to bring Melvin Adams's name to the police on a silver platter.

At this point, the determined Marion Jayne decided to step in and help out the Illinois Bureau of Investigation (IBI). She offered to approach Adams, offer the reward and appeal to his sense of fairness. The IBI agreed to it, and Marion arranged a meeting between Adams, his girlfriend and herself. Marion arrived at the meeting with a bag filled with $25,000, which was the exact amount of the reward she was offering. She offered the reward to Adams and his girlfriend. She begged him to go to the police and tell them who had killed George.

Melvin Adams had been a wild child. He had pulled a gun on a man. He was sure that he would be able to kill a man. However, when that became too much, he discovered he had a conscience. He decided he did not want the reward money. With Marion's plea, he finally caved. After refusing to take the money, he arranged to speak to investigators.

The IBI, meanwhile, was making progress in its own investigation. They tracked down Edward Nefeld, and he also began to talk.

Silas had been certain that he had bought and threatened the silence of the people he had hired to do the deed he had been attempting for ten years. He was finding out that loyalty was a lot harder to keep than he had thought. His minions began speaking like trained birds to any investigator who would listen.

Nefeld told the IBI about the contract Silas had put out on George. He also confirmed that he had originally accepted the contract but passed it along to Adams. Meanwhile, Adams was telling his own story.

Several weeks after the murder, the police had enough evidence and witness testimony for arrest warrants. They arrested Adams, Barnes, Nefeld, Silas Jayne and one other of Silas's men, Joseph La Placa. Barnes was charged with murder and conspiracy, and the rest were charged with conspiracy to commit murder.

Silas hired himself one of the most famous lawyers in the country. F. Lee Bailey was famous for defending the man who would become known as the Boston Strangler. He had defended other notorious criminals as well. Silas had enough money to hire the famous lawyer, who stated to the press that he felt the case against his client was, at best, thin. He was certain he would be able to provide evidence that would cast reasonable doubt and show that George had more enemies than just his brother.

Silas continued to talk to the press. He also continued to blame George's business dealings for his death. Silas stood in court and declared himself "100% not guilty."

Now began a short, but strange, trial. The local newspapers covered the trial with a strange kind of delight as the entire story of the feud between the two brothers grabbed headlines across the city. Many people who had no idea about horses and horse shows suddenly knew that a criminal empire had been run in the suburbs of Chicago.

Prosecutors trotted out their witnesses. A steady stream of misfits and malcontents, all of whom had found themselves in the orbit and influence of Silas Jayne, crossed the witness stand. Despite Silas's cold eyes and deathly stares, nothing could stop the avalanche of evidence that spilled from their lips.

All of the defendants were found guilty. All of them were ultimately convicted. After what F. Lee Bailey would declare was "the most bizarre murder case I've ever seen," his client was sentenced to prison for hiring men to kill his brother. The trial lasted all of thirty days.

Julius Barnes, the man who had crouched outside of George's home and fired a rifle into his chest, was sentenced to fifteen to thirty-five years for murder. La Placa, who had helped pass money along to the various players, was convicted and sentenced to six to twenty years in prison. Silas Jayne, meanwhile, was convicted and sentenced to six to twenty years for conspiracy to commit murder.

Silas was sent off to the Vienna Correctional Center to serve his sentence. According to those who visited Silas and saw how he spent his time in prison, Silas did not have a hard time behind bars. He was allowed to ride horses around the prison grounds. Some say he was even able to charm the guards enough that they allowed him to ride his horse into the nearby town and conduct business. Silas would end up serving only seven years in the correctional facility.

Most importantly, Silas was visited constantly by the men who were in his "gang." He was given regular updates on scams and schemes he had started before going off to prison and then came up with more while he was in prison. He maintained a rigid control over his empire despite being in prison. In fact, he may have been involved in one more of the most notorious crimes in the history of Chicago.

Silas had a tendency to bring men who were looking for a father figure under his wing. He taught these lost souls how to run his scams. He kept in contact with these people and helped them run more scams, but many of them also ran their own. It was one of these men who may have come to Silas for advice on what to do with a wealthy woman he had scammed money from. Her name was Helen Brach, and she had inherited millions from the Brach candy fortune her husband had managed. She had suddenly disappeared. Silas was believed to have been the mastermind behind it.

It would be Silas's final scam. However, it would leave a mystery that lasts and is still talked about in Chicago lore to this very day.

CHAPTER 4

THE CANDY WOMAN

Helen Vorhees Brach was born Helen Vorhees on November 10, 1911. She was not born into wealth. Her family lived a very working-class existence. She lived a relatively normal and uneventful life for about forty years, and then, rather suddenly, her life became something for the history books.

Helen had gotten married when she was young. Like most women of that time, it was sort of expected that she would marry young and start a family. She had no children with her first husband, and the marriage eventually ended for a variety of reasons. Soon, Helen Vorhees found herself living in Florida and looking for a job. She found one as a hatcheck girl at the Palm Beach Country Club.

Throughout her life, Helen had a love of animals. She had numerous pets when she was growing up. However, she had a love of horses in particular. She longed to own numerous horses and to ride them and watch them ride in fields she owned. She finally found a man who could provide her with that dream when she met a man who was a member of the Palm Beach Country Club and who also happened to be someone who was feeding America's sweet tooth.

Emil Brach came to the United States with a desire to bring candy to children. He set up a shop in Chicago to sell candy that he made by his own hand. He also had a recipe for making little squares of caramel that would soon become a signature of the Brach Candy name. He had discovered that baking, rather than boiling, the caramels gave the candy a deeper and richer flavor. Soon, the candies were a hit, and his little candy stand was in demand.

As successful as Emil was, however, he was content with simply running his candy store. When Emil finally left the business, he left it to his son, Frank Brach. Frank had ideas to take the candy out of the one shop in Chicago and put the Brach candies in stores across the country. He took his idea and ran with it, and soon, he was worth millions and the Brach Candy name was known all over America. Stores carried the famous bins of candy of all sizes and flavors. Brach Candy became one of the biggest candy makers in the country.

Frank Brach met and married a woman—again, much like it was expected that he would. It was also expected that he would have children to produce an heir to the Brach Candy throne somewhere down the road. That did not happen. The marriage eventually turned sour, and Frank found himself in the middle of a major domestic crisis while also trying to manage a multimillion-dollar empire that was growing all the time.

One of the things Frank liked to do was golf. He liked to spend time in the air and in the sun. One of his favorite places was the Palm Beach Country Club. In the midst of the turmoil and the hassles going on in his personal life, Frank made a journey to Florida that would change his life. Reportedly, it was love at first sight.

That fateful day, Helen Vorhees was working as a hatcheck girl, as she normally did. The money wasn't great, but the work was steady and regular and she got to meet some interesting, and wealthy, people. By all accounts, she was a nice person, not someone who was out to nab a rich man. However, when she looked into the eyes of Frank Brach, a man much older than she was, she was smitten. The same was to be said for Frank. His heart was hers from the moment he locked eyes with her.

Frank humbly asked the beautiful hatcheck girl out on a date. She accepted. He told her about his marriage and that he was still married. He also told her about how the marriage was falling apart. She stated that she didn't care, and they started a very passionate love affair. Frank admired her spirit, her willingness to help people and her love of animals.

The divorce moved forward, much too slowly for the taste of the two lovebirds. However, the divorce was finally finalized. Frank put his affairs in order and then headed back down to Florida. He asked Helen Vorhees if she wouldn't mind becoming Helen Vorhees Brach. It was only a few months after his divorce, but it was not much of a surprise to anyone who knew them. Helen said yes.

By all accounts, Frank and Helen Brach were perfect for each other. Despite the difference in their ages, the two were like teenagers. Helen was in her forties and Frank was in his sixties, but they acted like they were in high school. Frank continued to make the Brach Candy name a household one while Helen took to her new life of riches.

Frank and Helen Brach had an estate in Glenview, Illinois. It was a large house for the two of them. One other person who was also in the house most of the time was the houseman, John Matlick. He had worked with Frank's father, and Frank sort of inherited the handyman. Matlick lived in a home in Schaumburg that was also owned by the Brachs and worked during the day maintaining the Brach house and helping run things around the estate.

Helen was a meticulous and lifelong journal keeper. She had hundreds of books filled with her thoughts and ideas. She wrote in her journals every single night. She recorded everything she did and thought in those pages. By the time she met and married Frank, she had thousands of pages written.

Helen liked being a woman of means. She liked having clothes and cars. She liked her pink Cadillac. She also liked having pets and animals. She liked being able to travel where and when she wanted. She also began to develop her quirks. She liked animals, but she also liked wearing furs. Helen liked spending money lavishly on her friends and family. She thought nothing of buying expensive gifts for her brother, Charles, for example. Charles was working hard for a railroad line far from Helen and far from his home. She also liked to buy expensive gifts for her friends. However, she also had a habit of fretting and fussing over seemingly insignificant expenses.

When it came to her beloved pets, in particular her dogs, there was no expense too great. Helen would do anything for animals. She set up the

Helen Brach Foundation with the express purpose of funneling money to various animal causes. One story in particular showed her devotion to her animals and how far she would go to keep them safe and secure.

Frank and Helen had decided to spend some time in the Bahamas. She packed up her dogs, and they flew to the islands, enjoying time in the sun and surf. However, one of her dogs got sick. She didn't trust the airlines to get her dog back. She also had a particular vet whom she trusted and wanted only him to see her precious pet. So Helen Brach chartered a plane, for thousands of dollars, and had her pet flown back home so it could visit her favorite vet. She also cut short her vacation to make sure the dog was taken care of.

Frank and Helen were wealthy, and they enjoyed the life of the wealthy. They had a big house, and they went on expensive vacations and both had expensive clothes. However, they were not the type to play with the jet set in the Chicago area. Helen had some very close friends whom she talked to on the phone, sometimes for hours at a time, every day. Many of these friends were ones she had before she met Frank and long before she had millions of dollars at her fingertips.

Frank and Helen lived a very happy life together for twenty years. While Frank's previous marriage had fallen apart, there are no indications that there was any strife or problems with his marriage with Helen. Then, in 1970, Frank Brach died suddenly. He left Helen alone, heartbroken, but with a fortune of about $20 million at her disposal.

Helen was a woman who was meticulous with certain things. When she traveled, she always bought her tickets ahead of time. She also always called her friends and let them know every part of her agenda. She always let people know where she was, especially after Frank died. She kept close to her tight circle of friends and kept in even greater contact with them once she was alone.

Helen had millions of dollars at her disposal. She had a huge house and estate. She had John Matlick as her houseman. She was alone and had no job, few friends and lots of time on her hands. She had an almost fanatical desire to help animals. According to those who knew her, she loved animals more than she loved most people. Finally, and probably fatally, she loved horses. In Chicago, having a love of horses, particularly show horses, could put you in contact with very dangerous people.

As Helen got older, she got into stranger and quirkier things. For example, in addition to her obsessive journal-keeping, she got into something called "automatic writing" or "spirit writing." This was a type of spiritualism that involved the medium dropping into a trance and summoning spirits. The spirit would "take over" the body of the medium, who would then write, the hands and pen controlled by the spirit. Sometimes these writings were supposedly prophetic in nature. Helen would have regular "spirit writing" parties, and she began visiting a local medium on a regular basis. In fact, she began contacting her medium frequently for advice about when she should travel and other business decisions.

Richard Bailey was born with a very strange condition. He was born with eyelids that didn't open the right way. This strange condition required him to walk with his head tilted back just so he could see where he was going. This led to lots of torment from his classmates and other kids when he was growing up. When he was an adult, he had the condition fixed, but the mocking he had endured when he was younger stuck with him. It made him angry.

The condition had a lasting effect on his appearance even after he had the problem fixed. It made his face appear as though he was emotionless at times. His eyes were still half-lidded, as though he were sleepy or about to drift off and take a nap. It made him look somewhat bemused, even when tales of the things he had done were being told back to him in court.

When Richard Bailey eventually became an adult, he got into the world of horses. He eventually owned and operated Bailey Stables and Country Club Stables. He bought and sold horses to the wealthy. Of course, this line of work would bring him into the orbit of Silas Jayne and the Jayne Gang.

Exactly how much influence Silas Jayne had over Richard Bailey is open to debate to this day. Private investigator Ernie Rizzo, who was hired to look into the Brach case, claims that there was little influence. Rizzo says the two men may have done business, and likely did do business, but did not get along with each other. There are others who have looked into the case who claim that Silas found and mentored Bailey when he was still fairly young and new to the horse business. What is known, and admitted to by Bailey, was that Silas Jayne and Richard Bailey did business together when it came to buying and selling horses. In fact, Bailey had many contacts in the horse world across the country. What is also known is that Bailey's scams with horses bore a striking resemblance to the scams run by Silas and his gang.

Richard Bailey liked to scam women. While Silas Jayne had a predilection toward young women and preyed upon parental guilt, Bailey liked to prey on older women. Bailey would put ads in the newspapers or would meet these women through his stables, and then he would pounce. If he found out that the women had lots of money and were single, he would turn on the charm.

To the horse world, Bailey was considered a shady character. He wore cowboy boots and hats even in the Midwest. He was made fun of behind his back. He still had his half-lids and strange eyes. There were rumors that he mistreated or even brutally abused the horses in his care. However, he had a way of pushing aside those accusations and running his scams.

Bailey would swoop in on these old and lonely women. Many of them were widowed, and most of them were sick and full of health problems. He would sometimes get power of attorney from them and then have full access to their money. Other times he would look for their weakness. If he found out that the woman had a taste for alcohol, he would buy her champagne and alcohol. He would prey upon these women like a parasite and romance them. He would provide them with the companionship they were craving and cause them to fall head over heels in love with him. Then he would really start working his scams.

Sometimes he would just get them to give him money. That was the easiest thing and usually how things started. However, at some point, if he hadn't already met them at his stables, he would take them to his stables and show them his horses. He would concoct a story about his need to buy a particularly valuable horse that would be worth a fortune. He would get these women to give him money or, more often, secure a loan for him. Many times, he would use people he had recruited for his schemes and the horses would be wildly overvalued. The horses he claimed were worth many thousands of dollars were worth maybe half the amount he claimed he needed.

Bailey would start to drain them dry. He would default on the loans, so the women he had scammed were on the line for the care, stable fees and other expenses that went along with caring for a horse. They would continue to pay, feeding money into the ever-hungry Bailey machine until he felt that they were either catching on to his scams or likely to be out of money, and then he would leave them.

Bailey left a long line of old, broken and broken-hearted women in his wake. Most of them were too embarrassed to report Bailey. Many of them were afraid of what he might do. So Bailey began to think of himself as indestructible.

So it was in this world that Helen Brach eventually found herself. She was exactly the kind of woman that Bailey found as his perfect target. She was old, lonely and alone, and she had a deep love of horses. It was as if the two were meant for each other.

Helen Brach lived in her mansion and tended to her animals. She wrote extensively in her journals. She spent hours and hours on the phone talking with her friends all around the country. She devoted herself to the Helen Brach Foundation. She made occasional appearances at fundraisers and other activities, but she did not hobnob with the other wealthy in Chicago. She had her houseman and she had her pets. She had a reputation of being slightly eccentric, but she was not considered crazy. She was known as the "Candy Lady" or the "Candy Woman." Generally, she was well liked.

Helen still liked to lavish her friends and family with gifts. She liked to spoil her brother, Charles, although he was hardly living the life of the wealthy like his sister. He still worked for a railroad company and was looking forward to retiring.

Helen was in pretty good health in February 1977. Like many of the wealthy in the country, she was a regular patient at the Mayo Clinic in Minnesota. She wanted to be treated by the best doctors the country had to offer, and the Mayo Clinic had a reputation for having the best and the brightest in the medical field. It was a well-earned reputation. Helen decided it was time to have a checkup that February and made plans to visit her doctors in Minnesota.

Helen was also making plans to visit law enforcement sometime in the near future. She had been dating a man named Richard Bailey. He had wined and dined her and made her feel special. Perhaps not as special as Frank had made her feel, but he had made her feel younger and happier than she had felt in a while. Plus, he owned horses and bought and sold horses. However, Helen Brach was not nearly as gullible as many of Bailey's previous victims. She still had her wits about her, and she was familiar enough with animals to know that the ones Bailey was trying to get her to buy were worthless. She also had heard from others that Bailey abused animals, including the horses she wanted to buy. She was getting ready to expose Bailey and his scams. However, she wanted to make sure she had everything in order before she did it. That included a clean bill of health from her doctors.

So at the end of February 1977, Helen Brach phoned her friends and told them she was flying to Minnesota. She planned ahead, got her plane tickets and told her friends her itinerary. She then had her houseman, John Matlick, drive her to the airport. She took off and landed in Minnesota and was seen by witnesses. Despite Matlick driving her everywhere and being her constant companion since the death of her husband, he did not go with her to Minnesota.

Helen showed up for her appointment with her doctors at the Mayo. She was told she was a little bit overweight but otherwise she was in perfect health. She had some minor tests run, and everything appeared to be in proper order.

The Mayo Clinic is a very exclusive place that caters to a very exclusive clientele. Near the clinic is a hotel. Since the Minnesota winters are notoriously cold and certain clientele did not want to have to walk the streets in that cold, the hospital built a tunnel that connected the hotel to the hospital. This tunnel is the last place where anyone was certain they saw Helen Brach alive.

Helen walked through that tunnel to the hotel. She had plans to head back to Chicago that Thursday. She stopped in the hotel gift shop and purchased a few items. While she was checking out and paying for the items, she reportedly said to the clerk that she was "in a hurry" and that her "houseman" was waiting for her back home. This would become a source of contention during the investigation, but the clerk was certain the term she used was "houseman." Helen Brach seemed to simply vanish from the face of the earth after that moment. No one could be certain, after that point, if she was alive or dead.

John Matlick had a version of what happened to Helen. He didn't report her missing until days after she was supposed to return from her trip to the Mayo Clinic. Then he contacted the police and gave them a story that immediately put him at the top of the list of suspects.

According to Matlick, Helen Brach came back from the Mayo Clinic when she was supposed to. He claimed to have picked her up at the airport. Normally, Matlick stayed at the mansion when Brach was out of town. When she was back, he returned to his house, also owned by Brach, in Schaumburg. This time, however, he called his wife and stated that he had work to do at the mansion and he was staying the weekend at the mansion to get some remodeling and work done on the house.

Matlick stated that Brach returned on a Thursday and stayed through the weekend. However, despite her tendency to call her friends and family and spend hours on the phone, she didn't call a single person. She called no one about her trip, about her doctor's appointment or about plans she was making to travel anywhere else. Matlick stated that she had plans to visit friends in Fort Lauderdale, Florida. However, despite her previous tendency to obsessively call her friends and family about her trips, she called no one about this. Despite the fact that she always bought her tickets beforehand and was obsessive about her itinerary, she didn't buy her airline tickets that weekend. She spent no money using her credit cards that weekend either.

Matlick's version of the story is that on Monday morning she asked him to drive her to the airport. He reportedly drove her to the airport before 7:00 a.m. and dropped her off at the airport. She had packed no bags. She, according to Matlick, had brought cash to pay for her ticket at the airport. However, there were no flights to Fort Lauderdale anywhere near the time Matlick told authorities he had dropped her off. She would have had to wait for at least three hours before there was a flight.

No one was called when the first flight to Florida landed. She called no friends. She did not arrange for anyone to pick her up. She called no one to tell them she had traveled and had landed safely. There was just silence.

Matlick, however, had checks that he claimed were written to him and signed by Brach. The total number of checks he had totaled about $15,000. He also was still working at the mansion. He called and had contractors come in and put down new carpet and paint one room in the house. He demanded that they come immediately and do the job as quickly as possible. Then he began making purchases that seemed strange. First, he began calling several different outlets of a local department store. He called three before he found what he wanted. He ordered a meat grinder attachment to a food processor. This would become a source of much speculation later on.

Days after he reportedly dropped Helen Brach off at the airport, he finally called police and reported her missing. The police found Matlick to be very cooperative—almost too much. But his story had holes in it that they could not fill, and neither could Matlick. However, they also had no body. They had only a missing person and a story saying that she was alive and well and in Florida.

As authorities probed deeper, they just found themselves with more questions and little evidence. About two weeks after reporting that Helen Brach was missing, and with no body and no confirmation that she was dead, Matlick contacted her brother, Charles Vorhees. Even though he had told authorities that, as far as he knew, Helen was alive and well in Florida, Matlick told Vorhees to come down to Brach's house right away. Even more surprisingly, Vorhees did exactly that.

What happened next would leave authorities and investigators scratching their heads for years. Vorhees and Matlick spent time in the mansion, searching the house. Then, according to Matlick, he told Vorhees that Brach had informed him that, should anything happen to her, he was to burn all of her journals. Surprisingly, Vorhees agreed, and the two men burned every single journal that Helen Brach had written over the years. All of the information that was contained in her journals and journals filled with supposed "spirit writing" went up in smoke and flames.

At stake was about $21 million. At first, there was no will to be found. Brach's attorneys began searching the house, and they kept coming up empty. Then, suddenly, during a search of the house in April, the two men found a suitcase in the middle of Brach's bedroom. Inside the suitcase was her will, which had a late amendment attached to it that gave John Matlick $50,000. Vorhees was entitled to $500,000 that had been kept in a trust Brach had set up for him. His days of working for the railroad would be over with that wealth.

Again, the authorities didn't believe a word of what Matlick was saying. However, again, they were flummoxed. They had no body. Although Matlick stood to inherit money, it would be seven years before he could collect because, without a body, Brach would have to be gone for seven years to be declared dead. It didn't make any sense. They then began to check into parts of his story that seemed to stand out.

First, they confirmed that he had, indeed, hired contractors to come out and rework a room in the mansion. They had repainted the walls and laid down new carpet. However, the contractors claimed they had seen nothing unusual in the room and nothing that seemed to indicate any foul play.

Second, the entire city seemed to worry about the meat grinder. Investigators and the public had the image of Helen Brach being brutally murdered in her own home and then ground up and fed to her dogs. However, the police viewed the grinder and found it to be far too small and puny to grind up human flesh and bone. It was really just a machine for grinding meat to make sausage. It would have been impossible for the grisly task many had imagined.

Third, they asked Matlick about the forged checks. Specialists had viewed the handwriting and compared it to samples of Helen Brach's, and they all confirmed that she had not written the checks or signed them. Matlick claimed she had injured her hand on a suitcase while packing and had been forced to write the checks with her left hand. Again, authorities did not believe this. However, they also compared the writing to Matlick's, and again, it was not a match. Matlick also stated that Brach often let him sign checks for her in order to pay for things around the house. The police got this confirmed by others.

So authorities were, again, backed into a corner. They had no body. They had no evidence of foul play. Records and journals had been destroyed. Brach had not used her credit cards, and no one else had either. They had a man who had some forged checks, but they were more concerned with the possibility that they had a very dead candy heiress to find.

The authorities and Brach's estate got permission to release a reward. The first reward was for $100,000, and it was for any information that led to Helen Brach either dead or alive. They hoped that the floodgates would open and tips would come pouring in. Instead, the investigation ground to a halt. There was a large amount of money at stake, however. Brach's attorneys now had control of the money until such time as she was declared dead. Once that happened, Matlick would get his $50,000 and Vorhees would have access to half a million dollars.

The case stayed in the minds of investigators and the public, however. Newspapers ran stories over the years in which they would rehash the story of Matlick and the candy heiress. Matlick kept working at the estate for some time before Brach's lawyers finally released him from his job. He was also kicked out of the home in Schaumburg. Matlick led a very quiet life at that point, just waiting for the time when Brach would be declared dead.

However, one of Brach's attorneys was determined to find out what had happened. He had a fortune at his fingertips, and the time was counting down to when that money would have to be released to the people in the will. So he started calling people in to tell him what they knew.

Matlick came in and told the same story he had told authorities. He told the tale of sending the elderly candy heiress off to the airport so she could fly to Florida. He claimed he had no idea what had happened to Brach after that and had no reasonable explanation for the forged checks or the amendment to the will.

Then, while looking through records that had escaped the fire, the attorney came across the name of Bailey. Puzzled, he started asking around. He found out that Bailey and Brach had had a brief romance at one time. So he called Bailey into his office to explain what had gone on and ask him if he knew anything about Brach's disappearance.

What the attorney saw that day left him wondering if someone else might be involved in the disappearance beyond John Matlick. Bailey showed up with an attorney of his own. He refused to answer questions. He declared himself unwilling to answer under the Fifth Amendment, which prevents a defendant from testifying against himself. He refused to acknowledge that his name was Richard Bailey. Finally, he refused to acknowledge that he knew Helen Brach at all. As he left, the attorney was confused, puzzled and more convinced than ever that Helen Brach had met a very nefarious end.

However, with no body and no further evidence, things sat for seven years. The reward was raised to $200,000 for information leading to Helen Brach, dead or alive, but the increase in the money did not bring about any more evidence. It was as if Helen Brach had simply vanished from the face of the earth. She was gone, but the public, and her friends, still wanted to know what had happened.

Detective Ernie Rizzo was hired by a close friend of Brach's to look into the disappearance. Rizzo focused on Matlick. Matlick seemed to be the most guilty looking. He seemed to be the one with something to gain. Rizzo became convinced that the entire murder was one of passion and that the money in the will was, at best, secondary.

Matlick, meanwhile, was keeping a low profile. He was not asking any judges to release money to him any earlier. He was not making any waves. Everyone was just waiting.

At one point, the bones of an elderly woman were found in a forest preserve on the North Side of Chicago. The initial thought was that the body of Helen Brach had, at last, been found. The newspapers were abuzz with the story of the body. However, not long after, it was stated that the body was the wrong size. The bones were that of a smaller woman than Helen Brach. Also, the skeleton had no teeth, and Helen Brach still had hers. It was not the body of Helen Brach, and the mystery continued.

Not long after the skeleton was found, a tip came in stating that Helen Brach had been buried in a pauper's grave on the South Side of the city. Acting on the tip, investigators found the burial site. Again, with the Chicago media looking on in great anticipation, the grave was dug up and the skeleton removed. Once again, however, DNA tests showed that this was not the body of Helen Brach.

In early 1981, two psychics contacted authorities saying they had had visions that Helen Brach's body had been dumped in the Lake Kegonsa State Park in Wisconsin. Although authorities were doubtful, they had nothing else to go on. So the police spent hours and dedicated resources to searching the state park. They came up empty.

Other rumors began to surface about the relationship between Helen Brach and the mysterious John Matlick. Some suggested that they might have had a romantic relationship. However, investigators quickly ruled this out. By all accounts of Helen's friends and others who had any contact with either Brach or Matlick, they were simply employer and employee. This, of course, raised doubts about whether Brach had willingly added the amendment to her will giving Matlick so much money.

The years went by, and the mystery deepened. Ernie Rizzo gave an interview early on stating that a mysterious woman would occasionally answer the phone at the Brach residence. Was this actually Helen Brach hiding? It turned out to be a maid hired by Matlick and quickly let go by the Brach estate.

Seven years went by. Almost immediately, Charles Vorhees contacted the courts and initiated proceedings to have his sister declared dead. Suddenly, the news of Helen Brach and the mystery of her disappearance was in the news again. Both sides began lining up witnesses to explain what had happened.

The judge declared that he did not believe Matlick's story. Under questioning, Matlick's story did not hold up, and the holes in it became obvious. He still clung to the original story he had told police early on, but when faced with the problems with his tale, he had no further explanations.

The judge talked to other witnesses. Richard Bailey once again denied knowing anything about the disappearance. He was not due to collect any money, and while his actions were suspicious, there was nothing the court could do. The judge was left to determine that it certainly appeared as if Helen Brach had died that fateful day in 1977 when she vanished from the Mayo Clinic. He declared Helen Brach deceased.

The next task was to determine the validity of the will. Again, witnesses were called. Brach's attorneys had objections and raised suspicions about the will. Ultimately, however, the will was declared valid. Matlick received his money, and Charles Vorhees now had control of a much larger fortune than he had originally been expecting. Over time, interest had been gathered on the money, and he was now better off than he had ever been before.

Richard Bailey was still on the investigator's radar screen, however. Before too long, the list of elderly, wealthy women he had scammed became too big. Some of them began complaining. Investigators began to probe, and when they did, they discovered the vast amounts of corruption within the horse world. Before too long, over twenty people were indicted for various forms of fraud involving horses. Among those names would be those familiar with the Jayne Gang, and the name Silas Jayne would emerge, yet again, despite the fact that the leader of the gang was behind bars.

As the investigators began to probe further and further into the mystery that was Helen Brach, some names began to surface. One of those was Kenneth Hansen. The other was Curtis Hansen. Some investigators began to wonder if they had something to do with Brach's disappearance. Before long, the name of Silas Jayne cropped up.

As it turned out, the probes into the Hansen brothers led to the discovery and solving of an entirely different case. Finally, the city had an answer to what had happened to three young boys back in the '50s. However, there was still the mystery of Helen Brach. They still had no body and no idea what had happened to the heiress.

Once investigators began probing and prodding those women who had been scammed by Bailey, the walls he had built began to come down. Soon, others started turning on Bailey. One man in Georgia who had been involved with horse scams with Bailey agreed to testify against the man in exchange for immunity. He told investigators how Bailey used his charms and abilities to find the weakness in his victims to gain their trust and ply their money from them.

Investigators found that Helen Brach had purchased roughly $300,000 worth of horses from Bailey. There were two theories about what had happened next. The first was that Brach realized the horses were not worth the amount of money she had paid for them and threatened to go to the police. The second theory was that Brach found out that Bailey had been abusing and mistreating horses, including her own, and that she was threatening to go to the police with that information. Some, it must be said, theorized that it was a combination of the two.

Faced with the accusations and mounting evidence, Bailey had little choice but to cop a plea. Many charges were filed against him, including fraud and the solicitation of murder in the disappearance of Helen Brach. He steadfastly denied having anything to do with Helen Brach or her disappearance. He admitted that he had scammed and defrauded thirteen women and copped to pleas for the fraud.

Bailey went on trial for soliciting the death of Helen Brach. The authorities went with what they had. They knew that Bailey and Brach had had a relationship. They knew that Brach had purchased horses from Bailey and that those horses were grossly overvalued. They knew that she had disappeared, and finally, they had at least one witness who had heard Bailey talking about Helen Brach. Her name was Pamela Milne, and she had been romanced by Richard Bailey. The two of them had gone out for dinner one night. During the course of dinner, to her surprise, Bailey admitted to her that he had been involved in the murder of Helen Brach. Milne had been afraid to come forward before now because she felt that Bailey would kill her. In fact, she wrote down what Bailey had said on the back of a payroll stub. She considered that payroll stub her "last will and testament." She told friends that if anything happened to her, she had likely been killed by Richard Bailey for what she knew about Brach's death.

Authorities were able to indict Bailey using charges they would normally use for mob investigations. They were able to declare that what Bailey was running was a criminal organization similar to the mafia. So they indicted Bailey under racketeering charges, which allowed them to charge him for past crimes, such as the Brach disappearance, and treat the case much like they would a mob trial.

Authorities ultimately indicted twenty-three people across the country. Most of them had business within the horse industry. All of them had participated in scams of selling and insuring horses that were greatly overvalued. Their scams had bilked thousands upon thousands of dollars out of elderly, wealthy women from across the country. They had left broken hearts and broken bank accounts in their wake.

By June 1995, both sides had presented their case. Judge Milton Shadur gave instructions to the jury, and the jury deliberated. Bailey was found guilty of fraud and for the disappearance of Helen Brach. Shadur then had to decide how much time to give Bailey. He had a choice of anywhere between two and a half years and life in prison. He ultimately decided to sentence Richard Bailey to thirty years in prison. Given that Bailey was in his sixties when the sentence was handed down, this was likely a life sentence.

That should have been the end of it. Of course, it wasn't. Authorities still did not know what had happened to Helen Brach. They still had no body. Yes, she had been declared dead, but where was the proof? They had managed to convict someone of her murder without a body, but the mystery of what happened that day still remained.

All of that changed in 2005. Bailey's attorneys filed motions to have his sentence dismissed. They claimed that they had evidence that Bailey had not committed the crime of murder, as had been implied. They also claimed they had evidence of what had happened that fateful day. A man named Joe Plemmons had come forward with information. Once again, the name was familiar to anyone who had spent any time investigating the activities of Silas Jayne. He claimed he had been there when the body of Helen Brach was disposed of. He also claimed that the Hansen brothers were involved in the murder and disposal.

According to Plemmons, Helen Brach never got on the plane in Minnesota. In fact, a woman was used as a stand-in to fill Brach's ticket. Helen Brach was grabbed and put into the trunk of a car by Curtis and Kenneth Hansen, who had been hired to eliminate Brach. They drove the car back to Chicago. Along the way, they attempted to kill Brach, wrapped her in a rug and stuffed her back in the trunk.

Plemmons stated that he was awakened in the middle of the night. The Hansen brothers were outside of his house, and they had guns. They told Plemmons what they had in the trunk and claimed that they had a way to dispose of the body; however, they had thought they heard the old woman moan from the trunk as they drove. They wanted Plemmons to finish her off.

Plemmons at first said no. The men opened the trunk, and he saw a body wrapped in a rug. He claimed that he saw no movement and heard nothing. He told authorities that he thought she was dead. Curtis Hansen held a gun on Plemmons, he said, and told him that if he didn't "put two holes" in the rug there would be two bodies wrapped up in the trunk. Plemmons took the gun and fired twice into the bundle. The men did not hear anything else from the body in the back of the car.

Plemmons was then put into the car and went along with the Hansen brothers to Indiana. At that time, there were still many active steel mills in northwest Indiana. They drove to one, and Plemmons helped the brothers remove the body from the trunk. They then placed the body in one of the huge furnaces in the mill, and Helen Brach's body was reduced to ashes.

This was Plemmons's story. Despite the tale, it was determined that Bailey had arranged for this to happen. It was his attorney's assertion that someone else, a different horse dealer, had ordered her death. The plea was not bought by judges, and Bailey's sentence was affirmed.

Over the years, the role of Silas Jayne in the murder and disappearance of Helen Brach has remained a debate. There are those who are convinced that he mentored and coached Bailey from the get-go and that, ultimately, he gave the approval for her murder and disposal. There was evidently enough evidence for investigators to start checking into what Silas knew, and there was some talk of indicting him or at least bringing him in for questioning. However, Silas escaped this by dying of leukemia.

Some have said that Silas did not get along with Bailey. Bailey certainly was not taken too seriously by people in the horse world. They treated him as if he was a fool. Perhaps Silas considered him a rival in the horse-scamming business. What is known is that Silas Jayne and Richard Bailey had done business together. They knew some of the same people. In addition, the scams they both ran were very similar.

Also linking them were Curtis and Kenneth Hansen. Also, Joe Plemmons had worked with and for Silas Jayne. When he gave his version of the story, Plemmons was certain that Silas Jayne had authorized the Hansens to remove Brach. In fact, one story says that the reason Plemmons was awakened that night was that Silas was worried Plemmons was going to squeal on him and it was a kind of test to see if he would remain loyal. Plus, if they had a gun with his fingerprints on it and had to turn in evidence against him, they could claim it was Plemmons who had killed Brach.

It is also widely accepted that prison was not much of a burden for Silas Jayne. He was given almost free reign to do what he wanted while he spent seven years in jail for the murder of his brother. Silas likely considered it a small price to pay for having accomplished his ten-year task of killing George. Silas's men made routine trips to see him in prison. Silas was also given as much time as he needed to talk on the phone. As such, business as usual continued under Silas while he was supposed to be incarcerated. He was even investigated, shortly after his release, for authorizing the burning down of a horse barn. There were other crimes committed by his nephew and members of his gang while he was in prison, and it was believed he was aware of all of it.

Silas was a man who asked for absolute loyalty. Those he felt were threats were bribed or eliminated. He maintained absolute control over his empire even from behind prison walls. It may never be known for certain what involvement he had in Helen Brach's murder. However, if Curtis and Kenneth Hansen really did have anything to do with it, it seems unlikely that he would not have known and would not have had to give his approval for them to do that. If they had done so without his approval, that would leave him open to risk that, should they get caught, they might be willing to turn against him.

To this date, no trace of Helen Brach's body has ever been found. Kenneth Hansen died in prison for the murders of the Schuessler-Peterson boys. Silas Jayne died in his sleep from an illness. Bailey still sits in prison. Curtis Hansen is also in prison for crimes he committed while working for himself and Silas Jayne.

Authorities believe that Helen Brach likely died because of her love of animals. She also died because she dared to get involved in the dangerous world of horses in the Chicago area. She dared step into the territory of a man who was notorious for ordering the deaths of people seemingly on a moment's notice. Her body may be long gone, and it is unlikely new evidence will appear at this point to answer the questions involving the mysterious disappearance of the candy woman.

CHAPTER 5

THE AFTERMATH

Silas Jayne sat in prison for conspiracy to commit murder against his brother George. By all theories of justice, that should have been the end of it, and him. He was given a particularly tough sentence, something admitted to by those involved with the case. Most of those who end up convicted of conspiracy generally get a two-year sentence. Silas had a lot more than that, and it was thought there were those who hoped he would die in prison. Silas was just too tough, too ornery and maybe a little too crazy for that. Still, he was leaving a landscape of destruction, murder, bloodshed, corruption and crime behind him as he sat in a prison cell.

An interesting thing began to happen as Silas sat in prison. Basically, anything that had anything to do with the horse world and involved crime was blamed on him, and connections between him and his crimes were sought. He had become so notorious that anything bad that happened to anyone he had ever done business with was blamed on him. Silas actually found this amusing, and he talked about it to the *Daily Herald* when he got out of prison.

In March 1979, a man named Earl Teets, his wife, Elizabeth, and his thirty-five-year-old son, Gary, were found shot to death in their home in Hoffman Estates. These days, that area is nothing but homes and condos, but in 1979 there was still enough open space there that the Teets family ran a farm. Earl Teets had bought horses from Silas Jayne. When his family was found dead, the authorities immediately began exploring any possible connection between the deaths and the Jesse Jayne Gang. No connection was ever found, but even in prison, it was assumed that Silas was arranging for people to die if they owed him money or they had committed any slight, real or perceived, against him.

Silas Jayne was paroled from prison in May 1979. He was still being investigated for a possible connection in the Teets family murder. He was also popping up regularly in the investigation into the Helen Brach case. There were those who thought he might have been involved in a bank robbery in a Chicago suburb. Also, there had been a mysterious fire that burned down a barn of a known rival of Silas's in the horse business. In fact, there were a series of barn burnings that Silas was suspected of arranging and being involved in. Also, there were rumors he had a list of twenty-four people he wanted murdered that he had compiled while in prison. Marion Jayne was reportedly on that list.

While he was in prison, Marion Jayne had brought a wrongful death lawsuit against Silas. The judgment had not gone well for him, and the judge ruled that he owed Marion $1 million. Despite having a Cadillac that he changed over ever year, wearing diamond rings on several fingers, wearing a belt buckle made out of a $20 gold piece and carrying his trademark money belt around his waist complete with $100 bills inside, Silas claimed that he had no money. He stated that his high-priced lawyer, F. Lee Bailey, had taken up nearly all of his money. He claimed he wanted to go back to work in the horse business. He stated that he and his nephew, Frank Jayne Jr., were going to start a new horse stable and get back into business. He claimed that if he were to do so, he would soon have his fortunes back.

There were problems with that plan, however. Since the wrongful death suit had gone against him, he was barred from making any money until the $1 million was paid off. So as soon as Silas got out of prison, he was back in court trying to resolve the issue of the money he owed.

Silas had appeared several times in the news even before he was released. He was reportedly a very good prisoner, charming the guards and prison officials. He had reportedly earned a furlough in 1978.

He was to be given a four-day leave from the prison. As soon as then governor of Illinois James Thompson heard about it, he admitted that he was outraged. He went on the local news and protested, and just as soon as Silas got home, he was brought back to prison and served out more of his sentence until 1979.

According to Silas, Thompson was the reason behind his stiff sentence. Silas told the *Daily Herald* that he had "Watergate-type information" about James Thompson. What this information was never came to light, and Silas never made any official public statement about it. He claimed, however, that he had had this information for years and that Thompson had hoped Silas would die while in prison. He also pointed to Thompson's blocking of his furlough as proof that the governor had it in for him.

Silas claimed that he just wanted to get back to work. In the two-page story for the *Herald*, Silas claimed that he had been offered $400,000 to write a book and help produce a movie about his life, but he had turned it down. He also restated his belief that George had been killed because he had been running horse scams. However, he now also stated that he believed George had been dealing drugs out of his stables and that possibly drug dealers had killed him. He also claimed that on the night Frank Michelle Jr. had been killed on his property, Michelle had fired first and shot Silas in the stomach.

Silas was indicted and brought to trial for the arson charges. Once again, the seventy-one-year-old Silas Jayne had to appear in court. Once again, the evidence against him was shaky, and he was acquitted. He raged in the newspapers, claiming that he wanted the truth to come out and accusing police of persecuting him. He stated that he would eventually prove he had never been involved in any crimes. However, he soon disappeared back into his home in Elgin, Illinois, with his wife.

In 1986, Silas Jayne was diagnosed with leukemia. There was no public acknowledgement of this. By this time, Silas had been out of the media for a while, although the investigations into the Schuessler-Peterson murders, the murder of Cheryl Rude and the disappearance of Helen Brach were still going on. In each case, the FBI and other investigators were looking at the name of Silas Jayne. Silas continued to deny any involvement.

Silas Jayne fought his cancer for a year. Then, in July 1987, he took a turn for the worst. He entered St. Joseph Hospital in Elgin and died later that day. He died quietly, according to reports from family. He simply drifted off to sleep and never woke up. It was not the kind of ending most people who knew about Silas Jayne would have predicted for him.

Once Silas Jayne died, investigators found that they suddenly had more leads in more cases than they knew what to do with. It turned out that most people were willing to talk now that they no longer had to fear Silas Jayne. With him gone, and his network of hit men and assassins suddenly without a leader, investigators found themselves with an abundance of people willing to talk.

Back in November 1980, the name of Richard Bailey was in the news again. He was accused, along with another man, of having beaten a man who ran a concession stand at a stable owned by Bailey and Harold Pick. According to the man, he rented space there and sold concessions and had fallen into debt. He claimed that Bailey and Pick took him into a private office and beat him severely. Bailey and Pick, he stated, claimed that he owed them $6,000. They ended up beating him severely and taking $2,500 that he had on him. Both Bailey and Pick were acquitted.

Silas Jayne ended up in the story because, reportedly, Pick was trying to sell his shares in the stable. He was reportedly trying to sell them to Silas Jayne. The horse stable had land over one thousand acres in size. Lawyers, however, blocked the sale, and Silas was frustrated again.

However, the name of Richard Bailey would not stay out of the media. After Silas died, it was revealed that Silas's nephew, Frank Jayne Jr., had introduced Silas to Bailey. In fact, it was revealed by Frank Jayne Jr.'s daughter that she had overheard her father and Bailey talking about how they needed to eliminate Helen Brach.

Of course, Bailey was eventually convicted in the Helen Brach case. However, there were, and still are, many who felt that Frank Jayne Jr. got away with murder. He would not, however, escape justice entirely.

The biggest case to get sorted out after Silas died, of course, was the Schuessler-Peterson murders. The investigation initially started into that of the Helen Brach case. As investigators probed that case, they began to shake loose evidence in the murder of the three boys. The city of Chicago was electrified as the most notorious unsolved murder case in the history of the city was finally solved. Kenneth Hansen was put in prison and died there.

However, other cases were still being investigated and had not left the minds of investigators. For example, the death of Cheryl Rude was still on the radar of ATF investigators. Now that Silas was dead and others seemed to be stepping forward to talk about other crimes, they thought that this would be a good time to probe that crime again. They focused on the actions of James Blottiaux.

Blottiaux probably thought he had gotten away with murder. Well, to be fair, he had so far. However, now the police focused in on his suspicious activities again. He had purchased that dynamite just before the bombing and had put in orders for more dynamite that he had never picked up. As the ATF began probing the witnesses and evidence available, they soon found a link between Blottiaux and the crime that was enough to bring an indictment.

Blottiaux was brought in for questioning about the murder in 1995. ATF agents brought him in for an interrogation that ended up lasting twelve hours. He was released at that point. It would be another two years before he was arrested and another four years before he would face a judge and a jury of his peers.

It was 1999, decades after the twenty-year-old girl had been blown to pieces while trying to move George Jayne's Cadillac. However, Rude still had family, and they wanted justice done. Also, there was no statute of limitations on murder in the state of Illinois. Blottiaux found himself on trial for murder. There was no one left to intimidate the jury. There was no one left with a money belt full of money to pay people off.

In July 1999, James Blottiaux faced the jury and stood in a courtroom while his sentence was read to him. He was found guilty and sentenced to two to three hundred years for murder. Finally, justice was brought against the people who tried to murder George and took the lives of people on the sidelines instead.

The Jayne family name was still tainted. Next in view was Frank Jayne Jr. There were still suspicious fires in various barns around Illinois and Wisconsin to be investigated. In particular, the police were interested in investigating a fire that had burned down the Northwestern Stables in which Frank Jayne Jr. was an owner. Investigators knew about the Jayne family tendency to burn down their own barns to collect the insurance money. Of course, there were those who figured Frank Jayne Jr. had gotten away with murder in the Helen Brach case. While this was hardly the same thing as murder, maybe they could put him behind bars, at least for a while. Years before, Jayne had spent some time behind bars when he was discovered selling cocaine at his stables.

Frank Jayne Jr. was indicted on charges of arson in the burning down of Northwestern Stables. Another Jayne was now on trial. He denied all charges, but the evidence was against him. In September 2003, Frank Jayne Jr. was convicted and sentenced to six years in prison for arson.

In July 2004, Frank Jayne Sr. passed away. Like Silas, he died quietly at the age of ninety-three. The last member of the original Jesse Jayne Gang was now dead. In fact, nearly every trace of the Jayne family was slowly disappearing.

In March 2005, Joe Plemmons came forward with his information about the Helen Brach case. Richard Bailey was back in court, this time claiming the statements from Plemmons cleared him of the crime. However, the judge determined that Bailey still intended to kill Brach and that meant he was still guilty. Bailey stayed in prison, and Helen Brach stayed missing.

In the aftermath of the years of Silas Jayne, the horse industry in the Chicago area suffered. The barns and stables once owned by the Jaynes were long gone; land developers had turned them into condos and other developments. As urban sprawl made land more and more developed farther and farther away from Chicago, the world of horses suffered.

The last of the Jaynes eventually vanished from the headlines and from the public consciousness. While other criminals even more notorious have grown famous in the Chicago area, the name of Silas Jayne has faded, despite the fact that his name appears, time and again, in some of the most famous crimes and murders in the history of the city. All that is left of the Jayne legacy is the memory of murder, bloodshed, fraud, broken lives and broken hearts. Their crimes nearly destroyed an entire industry. It has taken years for those who buy and sell horses to even start to get a modicum of respect again. However, as the memory of Silas's crimes has faded, faith in those who still work in the horse world has returned.

The Aftermath

However, Chicago is a city that seems to respect the criminals in its history. Al Capone is looked upon with a kind of awe. Although most people find the crimes of John Wayne Gacy and Richard Speck terrible, there is a certain element in the city of Chicago that still finds them fascinating. The name of Silas Jayne deserves to be ranked up there with those other names. His life was a long, strange, fascinating story of murder, mayhem and destruction, even among members of his own family. He not only destroyed those who crossed him but also felt no compunction or guilt about destroying people who just happened to be collateral damage. There are still missing people who may have gotten too close to the Jayne brothers' war, and the world may never know for certain what happened to them.

Silas Jayne is long gone now. However, his crimes will be remembered for a long time to come. The legacy of Silas Jayne lives on and will continue to do so for many, many years into the future.

BIBLIOGRAPHY

Aiken Standard. "Dark Horrors Haunt Horse World," Sunday, August 28, 1994.

Arlington Heights Herald. "Brother Is Charged with Murder Plot," October 1970.

Capettini, Roger. "George Drugged Horses, Cheated Buyers, Silas Testifies." *Herald*, Thursday, April 26, 1973.

———. "Silas Jayne Guilty of Murder Conspiracy." *Herald*, Monday, April 30, 1973.

Carpenter, John. "Brach Mystery Likely to Stay that Way." *Daily Herald*, Wednesday, July 27, 1994.

———. "Indictments Don't Mean Brach Case Is Solved." *Daily Herald*, Thursday, July 28, 1994.

Daily Herald. "BOMB: ATF Investigating Industry for More than a Decade," Thursday, December 18, 1997.

———. "BRACH: DNA Testing Could Solve Mystery," Wednesday, December 12, 1990.

———. "CRIMES: Barrington Site of Shootout with Baby Face Nelson," Sunday, February 21, 1999.

———. "Friend of Brach to Appear in Court," Friday, June 15, 1979.

———."Handyman Contradicts Testimony," Wednesday, May 28, 1984.

———. "Judge Grants Bail to Suspect in Decades-Old Murder Case," Sunday, December 24, 2000.

———. "Palatine Police Seek Clues in Jayne Slaying," Friday, October 30, 1970.

———. "Silas Jayne Dies," Sunday, July 19, 1987.

———. "Skeleton not Helen Brach," Wednesday, October 4, 1978.

———. "Teets-Jayne Link Under Investigation," Saturday, March 3, 1979.

———. "Tests to Determining if 'Pauper' Is Brach," Wednesday, December 12, 1990.

———. "2 Acquitted of Robbing Stable Concessionaire," Saturday, November 22, 1980.

Daily Register. "Promising Clue in Slaying of Three Boys Fades," Friday, October 28, 1955.

Dixon Evening Telegraph. "Suspect Teen-Gangs in Killings," Wednesday, October 19, 1955.

Duerksen, Susan. "Brach Died 7 Years Ago, Judge Rules." *Daily Herald*, May 24, 1984.

———. "Brach's Employee Lying: Lawyer." *Daily Herald*, Tuesday, May 15, 1984.

———. "Millions Riding on Brach's Death." *Daily Herald*, Tuesday, March 27, 1984.

Edwardsville Intelligencer. "Jackpot of Leads in Boys Killing," Friday, March 16, 1956.

———. "Vagrant Queried in 3 Boys Murder," Thursday, December 6, 1956.

Ginnetti, Toni. "Silas Jayne: 'I Just Want the Truth.'" *Daily Herald*, Monday, May 5, 1980.

Goodman, Leonard. "Kenneth Hansen." http://www.truthinjustice. org/kennethhansen.htm.

Gordon, Tony. "Stables Try to Erase Stains Left by Corruption, Investigations, Trial." *Daily Herald*, Tuesday, May 28, 1996.

Gribben, Mark. "Helen Brach: Gone But Not Forgotten." *Crime Library on TruTv.com.* http://www.trutv.com/library/crime/notorious_murders/ celebrity/helen_brach/index.html.

Herald. "Employee Last to See Brach Heiress," Wednesday, March 23, 1977.

———. "The Murder of George Jayne Described by Witnesses," Thursday, December 7, 1972.

———. "'Not Guilty,' Says Jayne," Wednesday, August 11, 1971.

———. "The Oddities Abound in Brach Case," Tuesday, June 7, 1977.

Januta, Laura. "Bailey Charming for His 'Prey,' Prosecutors Say." *Daily Herald*, Thursday, July 28, 1994.

———. "Judge to Decide Fate of Bailey Mystery." *Daily Herald*, Tuesday, June 6, 1995.

———. "1965 Bombing Caught Up in Horse Racing Scams." *Daily Herald*, Thursday, December 18, 1997.

———. "Note, Witness Claim Bailey Admitted Link to Brach Death." *Daily Herald*, May 31, 1995.

———. "Prosecutor Calls Version of 43-year-old Murder a Lie." *Daily Herald*, Thursday, May 28, 1998.

Journal-Tribune. "Court to Receive Will of Missing Brach Heiress," Thursday, April 13, 1978.

Korecki, Natasha. "Horseman Gets Six Years for Arson at Stables." *Daily Herald*, Thursday, November 13, 2003.

Kozak, David. "Appeal Delays Retrial Over 1955 Murders." *Daily Herald*, Wednesday, May 16, 2001.

Long Beach Press-Telegram. "Indict Man on Plot to Kill Brother," Thursday, July 1, 1965.

———. "$100,000 Reward Offered for 'Lost' Heiress," Thursday, December 29, 1977.

Manitowoc Herald-Times. "Coroners Jury Rules in Rude Bomb Slaying," Thursday, July 8, 1965.

Mausley, Bill, Jr. "Candy Heiress Remains Missing After 5 Months; Search Goes On." *Times Reporter*, Monday, July 11, 1977.

Montgomery, Diane. "Jayne Blames Politics for Prison." *Daily Herald*, June 10, 1979.

New Mexican. "$250,000 Offered for Information on Candy Heiress," Thursday, September 25, 1980.

Oakland Tribune. "Shot Ends Feud Between Brothers," Friday, October 30, 1970.

O'Shea, Gene. "Blood Feud." *Chicago Magazine,* 2006

————. *Unbridled Rage: A True Story of Organized Crime, Corruption, and Murder in Chicago.* New York: Penguin Press, 2005.

Palatine Herald. "Police Seek Clues in Jayne Slaying," Friday, October 30, 1970.

————. "Si Jayne Implicated in Brother's Murder," Thursday, June 3, 1971.

————. "State Drops Charge Against Silas Jayne," 1965.

"Renee Bruehl, Patricia Blough and Ann Miller, Disappeared from the Indiana Dunes State Park in Indiana on July 2, 1966." http://www. websleuths.com/forums/archive/index.php/t-25728.html.

Robinson, Mike. "Cop-Turned-Author Tells Story of Notorious Triple Child Murder." http://www.southcoasttoday.com/apps/pbcs.dll/article?AID=/20071118/NEWS/711180384/-1/NEWS02.

Rolling Meadows Herald. "Earlier Jayne Case Is Recalled," Wednesday, January 22, 1965.

Rozek, Dan. "Exhumed Body Just May Resolve Brach Mystery." *Daily Herald,* May 31, 1990.

————. "Georgia Man Suspect Pleading Guilty: Horseman Details Role in Scheme to Defraud Wealthy Women." *Daily Herald,* Thursday, September 8, 1994.

————. "Jayne's Part in Brach Case May Come Out." *Daily Herald,* Wednesday, July 27, 1994.

————. "Love for Animals May Supply Link in Brach's Disappearance." *Daily Herald,* Wednesday July 27, 1994.

San Antonio Light. "4 Charged in Death of Breeder," Sunday, May 23, 1973.

Schmalbach, Laura. "Brach Case a Mystery Forever?" *Sunday Herald,* February 18, 1979.

Smothers, David. "Is Heiress Dead? $50 Million in Limbo." *Elyria Chronicle-Tribune,* February 16, 1978.

————. "Strange Case of Helen Brach." *Salinas Journal*, Wednesday, June 8, 1977.

Southern Illinoisan. "Stable Owner Indicted," Friday, July 2, 1965.

————. "Survivor of Bomb Plot Is Slain," Thursday, October 29, 1970.

————. "Suspect Missing," Friday, October 30, 1970.

Taylor, Troy. Weird and Haunted Chicago. "The Schuessler-Peterson Murders." http://www.prairieghosts.com/spmurders.html.

Towney, Shamus. "Stable Owner Faces Arson Charges from Fire 17 Years Ago." *Daily Herald*, Friday, May 4, 2001.

Tyrone Daily Herald. "The Complicated Case of the Missing Heiress," Friday, February 16, 1979.

Van Wye, Joann. "Silas Jayne Makes 'New' Freedom Bid." *Daily Herald*, Saturday, July 19, 1980.